TANKS

short fiction

by

John Mort

BkMk PRESS-UMKC
College of Arts & Sciences

University of Missouri-Kansas City
5216 Rockhill Rd., Rm. 204
Kansas City, MO 64110-2499

Cover Illustration by Wayne Pycior who served in Vietnam 1969-70 in the 11th
Armoured Cavalry Division.

The novella "Tanks," which is included in this book was selected from
submissions throughout Missouri by Peter Meinke, well-known short story
writer and poet. As a result BkMk Press (University of Missouri-Kansas City)
with the help of the Missouri Arts Council, presented John Mort with $500 and
published the manuscript. We included a number of other Mort stories so that
readers could more fully sample the work of this talented writer.

missouri arts council

Financial assistance for this project has been provided by the Missouri Arts
Council, a state agency.

"Called of God," "Hot," "The New Captain," and an earlier version of "Gomez" have
appeared in Gentlemen's Quarterly, Missouri Short Fiction, Missouri Review, and Prairie
Schooner, respectively.

Library of Congress Cataloging-in-Publication Data

Mort, John, 1947-
    Tanks: short fiction.

    Contents: Good Blood—Called of God—Human Wave—(etc.)
    I. Title
PS3563.O88163T3   1985   813'.54   85-73391
ISBN   0-933532-55-5

BkMk Press

Dan Jaffe, Editor-in-Chief
Pat Huyett, Associate Editor

To Nathan, who had me up anyhow.

TANKS

Good Blood

"Looks like, if they was gonna have a war, they'd try to win it," Roy's father said.

"Oh, Jesus. Will you stop it? I don't wanta hear this!" They were out in the chickenhouse; the chickens were still sleeping. Down at the end, through the screen, Roy could see his Chevy, fading, forlorn by the dark woods. A huge ventilation fan cut up the sun's first rays, so that his father stood alternately in shadow and golden outline.

"It's this damned Johnson," said the old man. "You can't trust a Texan—"

"Just . . . don't talk. Please."

"Had a Texan working for me once, name a Phelps. Never sober. Now his wife, though, she was a good woman. Real pretty. Hard worker."

"Not like my mom?"

Roy's mother had gone to California with a man, when Roy was seven. Yet even this knife in the old wound wasn't enough to silence his father. Maybe the old man just talked to himself now, didn't really hear the replies. "Phelps got falling down drunk and beat her up. Pretty bad. She went home to Texas, and he moped around something awful. Only man I ever knew had eyes like a hound dog. Man couldn't help but feel sorry for him. Well . . . few months went by and he got religion. Swore off the bottle, and damned if he didn't talk her into coming back. Women are crazy. But there's what I mean about a Texan. Johnson would be all right if he'd kick that Kennedy bunch outta there."

"Oh, God. Shut up! You're so . . . ignorant."

His father blinked. Finally he bent to pick up his basket. "We better throw a little oyster shell, Roy. We been getting some soft eggs."

Roy eyed his father, neutrally, wondering if he'd really

1

silenced him. He hurried toward the feed room. He didn't mind the work, but it galled him, with the education he had, to listen to such foolishness. He set the bucket of oyster shell near the cages, picked up his own basket of eggs.

"You talk about respect," said the old man.

"I didn't!"

"I respect the man who does his duty. I know he's a friend of yours, but the Martin boy—"

"Duty! I just got trapped. I ran out of money, *Dad*. Duty!"

"Jim Martin lied, pure and simple."

"He convinced them. He wrote it nice. He just said . . . he objected to killing."

"Who don't? In my time they'd a throwed him in jail. Was a missionary's son in town, refused to go, they painted a yellow streak around his daddy's house. Awful thing. He had grounds, religious grounds! But—"

"I'm going to Canada," Roy announced.

His father nodded. "You won't. I'm gonna tell you why you won't."

"Not that. Not—"

"Because there's good blood in you. Good bull, he'll bring up the herd. You take, little runt of a bull, he's gonna bring it down, I don't care how nice your heifers are. You're like me, Roy, you—"

"Maybe I'm like my mother!" Roy spun like a discus thrower, moaning, ready as he might ever be to kill, and released his basket of eggs. They crashed into the wall and yolks slid down the calendar from Biggs Feed Mill, the one with the girl in pigtails. He ran outside. A wind had come up. It was cold.

The old man bustled about inside, making loud and improbable noises. Finally he came out, jingling his keys, looking into his billfold. "Let's get on the road," he said. "I'll buy you breakfast."

*   *   *

Polly Selznik, who at nineteen already had a kid, and already was divorced, brought their order. In high school Roy had never had the nerve to ask her out, but what he thought now was that he'd spent the entire summer working, lonely, when all the time he could have been seeing her. "Roy!" she said, smiling. "Answer

2

to a maiden's prayer."

He scanned her eyes. A different waitress had taken the order, and he wondered it there hadn't been a conference in the kitchen. "Hello, Polly."

"Roy's going into the service today," said the old man.

"I hope it's not because of a woman."

Roy slurped his coffee. "Drafted."

"I'm sorry." Polly shook her head. "What a shame, Roy."

"It is," said the old man. "This war don't make no sense. Explain it to me, Polly."

"I guess . . . I just don't pay much attention. Isn't that awful? I know someone over there, too. Get you fellas anything else?"

Roy looked at her carefully. "Might call you some time. When I'm home."

She laughed. "Thought you were interested in college girls."

"I'm interested—" He stopped, mindful of the old man at his elbow.

"I think Roy's pretty well done with school. Come right down to it, he's a farmer, same as me."

"You say!"

"He should finish up," Polly said. "Sure wish I'd gone."

"He wasn't serious, Polly! I said to him, engineering, even agriculture, that's fine. Welding. Business courses. But I told him, you're gonna go up there and paint pictures, by God you can pay for it."

"I got bad blood," Roy explained. "Runs in the family."

"Don't argue." Polly glanced toward a table where Butch Fredericks and Avery Dunn had taken seats. She sighed. "Listen, I'll bring you two some pie. My treat. Home-made, huh?"

Roy nodded. He wished he had time to fall in love. Strange, how lately, at completely unexpected moments, he found himself fighting back tears. He sat watching Polly as she hovered over Butch and Avery—in the National Guard, he remembered suddenly. He didn't have much of an appetite for pie.

*   *   *

The International rattled along, with an instinct for every bump. It was some incredible back route, and his father crunched

3

the gears with every shift. "Learn to drive," Roy said.

"Huh. I ain't put it out to pasture yet."

He meant the Chevy. Roy had gotten drunk one night, gone over redline, and blown the engine. The old man had towed it home. "That was four years ago. Give me a little credit, I—"

"We'll get her fixed while you're gone."

Roy couldn't speak. He'd been about to say that the old man couldn't let a sleeping dog lie.

They were in the city. The strange route had brought them in through the ghetto, behind delivery trucks, by a junkyard, over a hundred rail crossings. They sat at a light, and two tall black boys, pink combs stuck in their hair, were dancing in front of a pawn shop. Roy steeled himself for the inevitable racist observation: no matter how the old man goaded him, he'd be calm.

"Speaking of Polly," his father said.

"Please don't."

"Had some tough luck. Always mystified me, how these nice women settle on such hard cases. Guess there ain't enough good men to go around. But I'm gonna tell you something, Roy— woman like that, kid to think of, she'd stay with you."

"Hard worker, huh?"

His father didn't reply. As they pulled from the light, and the old man crunched his way into second, the two black boys stepped onto the street. They danced to some secret music, oblivious to traffic. Here it comes, Roy thought. The old man braked, and blundered back into first. But then they went on silently, a dozen blocks or more, over brick streets. An expressway curved parallel and then ran over their heads. Suddenly his father was backing the truck around. "I guess this is the place, Roy."

"Oh." Roy sat up. "Well . . . goodbye, then." Yet he didn't move.

"Same place they swore me in. Ain't changed a bit. Well—"

Roy looked through the rear window. A bus marked "Chartered" was parked under the expressway. A big sergeant stood before a group of twenty or so, in civilian clothes, in haphazard formation.

"I'm going," said Roy.

"The place is yours, Roy. It ain't like there's anybody else.

4

Make a farmer out of you yet."

"I don't want it!" Roy said. "I don't want that worthless place!"

"You may change your mind. Get over there—"

"What do you care? If I'm killed, if my legs are blown off, what do you care? You . . . drove me off!" Roy paused. He almost didn't say it. "Like my mother."

The old man hunched over the wheel. "Get on with you, Roy."

"All right! All right!" Roy opened the door and marched down the street. When he'd gone a hundred feet the sergeant looked up. He had a clipboard. "You belong here?"

Roy turned. His father rolled down the window, and waved, as slowly he gained speed. Roy nodded. He meant to shout out something, to wave. He rocked up on his heels, but his hands, it seemed, were paralyzed.

Called of God

When the helicopter dropped him off he just stood there, a sick grin on his face. He seemed too frail to hold up all the gear they'd loaded him down with. It looked like he didn't know where he was and never would know, and I kept hoping he'd be assigned to second squad. I didn't want him on my conscience.

Naturally, Lieutenant Klein sent him to me. So I shook his hand and told him to drop his pack anywhere. Make some coffee, cock up his feet, stay awhile.

"Yessir."

"What's your name?"

"Bobby Lee Daws."

"Well, Bobby Lee, this is the end of the line. You don't have to say 'sir' even to officers, and I sure as hell ain't no officer."

He nodded and plopped down in the dirt, his eyes held low. I gave him about two weeks. I patted him on the shoulder and said, "Just take it one thing at a time."

Then I grabbed my coffee and went up to see Klein.

Klein was smoking one of those little cigars and reading *Anna Karenina*. It was the longest book he could find. He'd been reading it for a month, all through the monsoon, and the glue had dissolved. He'd peel off pages as he finished, throw them behind us as we moved though the brush—gingerbread crumbs. "Thanks a lot," I said.

The lieutenant studied his cigar. "He's what they sent, Irish. Quality control ain't my MOS. Put him on point."

They called me Irish because in the mornings, to get going, I'd pour a little whiskey in my coffee. I'd do it in the evenings, too, to get stopped. "I don't know about the point, Butch. Man gets killed, it's right away. If we was to kinda watch over him for a while—"

"Shit," Klein said, flipping the cigar down into his foxhole, reaching for another. "If he's any good, he'll make it. Put him out

7

there, Irish. Baptism in fire."

*   *   *

When we took a break or camped for the night Bobby Lee
would read the Bible, holding it close to his face. On guard you
could hear him whispering prayers. "You a preacher?" I asked.
"I been waiting for the call." He said it like it settled
everything.
"What's *that*?"
"The Lord tells you, Irish . . . what you have to do."
"Huh. In a dream, like?"
"It can happen in a dream, but most times you hear this
voice."
"And this voice, it tells you to be president of the United
States or something."
"Even a garbageman."
"Well. I don't think I'd listen, Bobby Lee, if some voice told
me to be a garbageman. You ought to aim for truck driver, at
least."
He didn't smile. "Whether it's humble or mighty," he said,
very sternly, "the Bible tells us . . . to do what the Lord wills."
"Fuckin A," I said. Why not? It didn't matter to me if he was
in love with an elephant. The great surprise had been that he was
a good point man. Maybe it was because he was a country
boy—at home in the woods, cautious, alert in exactly the right
way. Anyhow, like a trance, six weeks of prayer and Bible
readings went by. Nothing much happened. Bobby Lee began to
seem like good luck.
I was walking second in thick brush. I got hung up in some
vines, and by the time I could work myself loose Bobby Lee
might have been fifty feet ahead. Nothing lonelier on earth than
for him to turn around then and see that I wasn't there. It was like
somebody had written the script. I heard two rifles firing, and a
scream.
We hit the ground. I eased off my pack, thumbed my rifle to
automatic and crawled forward on my knees. But it was the other
man who was dead. Bobby Lee stood looking out into the woods,
weaving slightly, like he was going to be sick. "Hey, man," I said.

The dead man was an officer. You could tell because the officers always wore Browning nine-millimeter pistols or one of those worthless Russian watches. Sometimes you could trade the pistols, which were Belgian-made and pretty, for a rear job. But this guy had had a watch. Karl Marx should have been on the dial, jerking his arms around.

Bobby Lee sat on the ground now, digging in the sand with a stick. I meant to cheer him up. "You got an officer, man! Headed him off at the pass."

He stared like he thought I was the devil himself. "I won't do that no more, Irish."

Klein poked his head through the leaves. "Real fine, real fine," he said, glancing over the scene. "An officer! Let me see that watch, Irish."

*　　*　　*

Sometimes a man would get a kill and turn cocky. He'd be more dangerous to himself and to everyone around him than if he'd just stepped off the plane. But I figured Bobby Lee was too meek to come down with blood-lust. He'd had his baptism in fire; I could stop worrying about him.

I even thought there was just the right balance in him, of caution and fearlessness, to make him the best man I had. When it was his turn to point again I was eating crackers and cheese, sipping my coffee and thinking soon I'd be home. Garcia came back along the file. "Irish. You know Bobby Lee, he don't have his gun."

"Huh?"

"He won't pick it up."

"No rifle?"

"That's what I fucking *said*, man." Garcia shrugged elaborately.

I stopped the platoon and grabbed the unclaimed rifle as I moved up toward the point team. Bobby Lee was sitting on his pack. "Here's your weapon, Mister."

"I don't want it."

"You think . . . your heavenly father will protect you?" Then I remembered. "Oh shit. Did you get the call, Bobby Lee?"

He didn't answer, and I tried again. "Listen, man: easy day.

9

Half a click to go—then we'll talk about it, okay? C'mon, let's go."

He shook his head. "It's the Lord's will, Irish. The Bible says, 'Thou shalt not kill.' It don't say you can kill in a war or something."

"Bobby Lee, you ignorant fucker! Listen, this is serious. This is—"

Klein buzzed me on the radio. "What's going on up there? You guys jacking off?"

*   *   *

The men sprawled out with cigarettes and cans of fruit. I had a headache: too much coffee, not enough crackers and cheese. Klein arrived, cigarless, with *Anna Karenina* poking out of his side pocket. "Problem?"

"Bobby Lee won't carry his rifle."

"Too heavy? Poor baby, he's tired."

"Doesn't want to kill anybody he says."

"Well, I don't either. Too fucking hot. I want to get set up for the night and read my book. That it? You overheated, Bobby Lee?"

"That's it," I said. "He's hot. Let me point into camp, Lieutenant. I don't mind."

Bobby Lee lifted his chin. "Nosir, I'm fine. I just ain't carrying no gun. I killed one man, and I been praying it through, and the Lord, he *said* to me—"

"He got the call," I explained.

"The what?"

"The call."

"Ah. The call," Klein murmured. He shook his head slowly. "Sergeant York."

"Who?"

"This old Tennessee . . . hillbilly, real religious, back in the First World War. Saw a light or something . . . decided he was a C.O. Crazy bastard. Bobby Lee—"

"Gary Cooper?" I asked.

"Right. Bobby Lee, listen. Go ahead and point, no weapon, it's your life. We hit the shit, you *know* whose ass is grass. You'll

10

be an ever-loving martyr, Bobby Lee. What is it, special place in heaven? Or are you just shamming it? You're scared shitless, troop, and you think this'll get you home. No way."

"I never said I wouldn't point, sir," Bobby Lee said. He rose and shouldered his pack. "I ain't trying to get out of nothing." He started to move forward.

"Lieutenant—" I began.

"Let him go, Irish."

"Butch, I tell you, he's serious. What if he walks into an ambush?"

"Never happen. Nobody's got that kind of nerve. You watch, he'll beg for that rifle. I give him five minutes."

It was like some guy in a wheelchair was our first line of defense. It was worse because you could tell Bobby Lee was no Daniel: He was scared and kept mumbling something. His fear drifted back and settled on every man's face. Maybe it was God's will that Klein didn't push too hard; we hadn't gone 200 meters before he signaled to make camp.

*   *   *

"The thing about Sergeant York," Klein said, "is that when it got rough, when he saw his buddies getting shot, he picked up his weapon and blew the fucking Huns away."

"Bobby Lee never heard of Sergeant York. Maybe not even of Gary Cooper."

"What am I supposed to do? This could ruin my career, Irish." It was dark by then. Around the camp, as if from a signal, every tiny noise ceased. Klein drew on his cigar.

"Better cup that light, Butch."

"Yeah. What's wrong with me, Irish?" He closed his hands around the ember.

"Nothing wrong. You just get to thinking you're a real person sometimes, instead of an officer."

"Well, up yours, troop. Why can't he act like everybody else? This is no tight ship. I don't want to come down on him."

"He's weird. Send him in."

"But how would it look? Lieutenant Ronald Klein turns soldiers into C.O.'s."

11

"Say he's nuts. I mean . . . he *is*."

It seemed like a good idea to me, but in the morning Klein strode over, looking grim, and shoved his face near Bobby Lee's.

"You *will* carry that weapon."

Bobby Lee looked like he'd cry. "Nosir."

"Nosir! We're not talking about a goddamn slap on the hands here, soldier. We're talking court-martial. You think that'll get you to the world? Not exactly. Long Binh Jail, troop. L.B. fucking J. Let me tell you, let me give you a little inkling, what it's like. You go to the first line, you come to attention, you salute. You say, 'Permission to use the latrine, sir.' You go to the next line. 'Permission to use the latrine, sir.' You get the idea, Bobby Lee? How fucking copy?"

"Solid copy, sir." His head bowed low. "But I *can't*. I can't carry my gun. I would go to hell."

"On your feet!"

He rose. We all were watching; we all had been in the same situation, where an officer, your friend, was suddenly an officer again, grinding you into the dirt. Yet it would have been over some prostitute or drinking on duty, not refusing to carry your weapon. Klein thrust the rifle forward, released it as Bobby Lee's arms rose involuntarily. Then the rifle fell to the sand. Shock waves went out into the jungle. Sacrilege.

"Sergeant!"

"Yessir!" I said.

"This man will point today."

"Yessir."

"I want you to take his water."

"Sir—"

The lieutenant glared.

"Yessir."

*   *   *

No air was moving and the trees themselves seemed to sweat; the distance ahead was murky and feverish, cut off by the oily, distorted sun. Bobby Lee reached around for the canteen that wasn't there. He fell, rose and looked toward me like he didn't know what he'd done wrong. I pointed toward Garcia, who was

12

carrying the disputed rifle. It seemed to make Bobby Lee angry. He rushed forward; a vine caught him and he spun violently, only to grow more entwined. I glanced back. Klein was watching, smoking; he murmured something to the second squad leader.

Garcia cut away the vines. Bobby Lee kept jerking; his helmet fell off and his hair looked like a wet mop. "Go easy," Garcia told him.

"I love the Lord!"

"Hey, hey, man," said Garcia. "This lieutenant is crazy. You ought to do it, man, a little thing. Take the weapon. You fall down, I know, he'll say, 'Piss on that soldier.' Everyone, we with you, man. You're right. But hey, man, he'll kill you. You'll die."

Yet Bobby Lee burst away, running a hundred meters and more. Then, in an open area, he staggered and plopped down in the grass.

"What's this?" said Klein, suddenly beside me. "He stopped in the open?"

"Give him a drink," Garcia said.

"I think we ought to, sir . . . give him a drink." I'd said "sir," and Klein dropped his eyes to me and paused, like he felt betrayed. "You miss the point, Irish."

"I don't miss the point, sir, but it won't work. He's too ignorant. Pretty soon he'll stroke out; we'll have to Medevac him. Send him back with the mail, sir."

Klein shook his head and hurried across the clearing. "Ready for a drink, Bobby Lee?"

His eyes were red and far away. He'd gone pale, except for where the vines had scraped his face and the blood puckered. He nodded.

"Garcia has your weapon, Bobby Lee. Pick it up, you don't have to point. Ever. You can carry ammo."

"Nosir."

"Nosir! You want to risk every man? My God! Then point, point! On your feet!"

Bobby Lee stood and tried a few more steps into the woods again. But in moments he collapsed against a tree. His head flopped and his body went slack and gray; he seemed pinned to the wood. The medic pressed salt water to his lips; Bobby Lee turned his head. "Drink, funkhead!" said the medic, and Bobby

13

Lee drank, again and again, as though brine were spring water. At last he smiled and his breathing slowed. No anger whatever: He stared off with a kind of fool's peace.

"On your feet!" said Klein.

"Lieutenant—" I began.

"Shut up! Soldier, on your feet!"

Bobby Lee tried to rise but couldn't. Klein knelt before him and shouted into his face. "We're leaving you here, you understand? Leaving you for Charley. Unless you take your weapon . . . here!" Klein shoved out the rifle. At first Bobby Lee seemed not to recognize it. Then he raised his hand and batted the stock away.

Klein never faltered. He stood, shouldered his gear and began walking. "Move out!"

He would not have abandoned Bobby Lee. He couldn't have gotten away with it; he'd have been the one requesting permission to piss. It must have been his final test, to move away a hundred meters or so and wait, to see if Bobby Lee would pick up the rifle and follow. Wouldn't he? Wouldn't anyone, left to die? Or would Bobby Lee have passed on into the exquisite pain of martyrs?

"No way!" Garcia screamed. "No *way*, Lieutenant!"

"No?" said Klein. "Garcia . . . no?" He looked at me, then, amazement on his face.

"Irish? You? No?"

"No, Butch," I said.

"No!" Garcia threw his rifle down. Behind him was a clatter, curses, as a dozen more threw down their rifles, too.

*   *   *

So—in the open place—we called for resupply. We read our mail and ate cookies from our aunts and maybe changed shirts. I had some whiskey. The sun went low, and Klein smoked cigars and sat staring at the last pages of *Anna Karenina*.

Garcia and I helped Bobby Lee onto the helicopter. Though I made a point of asking, I never heard of him again. Except for his one craziness, there was nothing special about him. You might have hoped he went from outfit to outfit, like a sort of Johnny

Appleseed, refusing to carry rifles. More likely, he spent ten months on KP.

As we began to move out again, I had the notion not to pick up my rifle. Just for a moment, and then I grabbed it, as always. I had only a month to go and didn't want to make any trouble, and when you come right down to it, I was never all that religious.

Human Wave

They'd broken through and been beaten back, come again, once more, and then the jungle and sea were silent. Perhaps the wind blew, moaning. Nolan, who hadn't been there, had visions of savage hordes, their scimitars high, their very souls crazed with opium. Anyhow he could smell the dead a mile downwind.

His company, a burial detail, had been dropped on this high dune, covered with stunted palms and mounds of red ants. They'd arrived before dawn, in a terrible whirl of urgency, and there had been some elaborate notion that they'd be attacking the enemy's flank. Now it was past noon, what remained of the enemy had fled, and Nolan stood looking out to sea, trying to keep the scent of salt in his lungs. The grey water merged with the grey sky. A quarter mile out was an island with palms and a temple; there was a ragged flotilla around the island, and, ashore, men were pulling in nets. The great Buddha stared down from his temple in golden dispassion, or anger, or joy. Near shore, some Australians were surfing.

Human wave! Scores of men, bound for hell or cradled in Buddha's arms—but who, what mind, could be alien enough to charge a machine gun? "Hundreds of them," Nolan murmured, as at last the company came down the dune, and divided into files on either side the road. Ahead, men searched the woods for wounded. "Hundreds," Nolan repeated.

"I heard they was gonna pour diesel fuel on 'em," Hennessey said. "Like you burn shit?" He was focusing his camera over the shoulder of the man ahead of him, and upon all the men in line, descending into the distance. He whirled and aimed at Nolan. "Only then the tv guys flew in."

Nolan tried to smile and yet keep moving, keep the rifle swinging. "Makes sense. If you're dead . . . what's the difference?"

"Naw, man. It was barbous!" The camera whirred; Nolan looked up. "You cain't put a thing like that on tv. So they flew in these 'dozers. To dig trenches. Nothing to it in the sand."

"Those bodies—"

"Hell, they come three nights in a row. Some of 'em been there almost a week now. I guess the gooks been trying to drag 'em off at night. Jeez. They gotta be ripe."

"They—"

Small arms broke out. Everyone hit the sand; down in the salty grass, Nolan lost all sense of where Hennessey was. He was afraid to call out. Once before this had happened: lying in the sun, he'd pissed his pants, but was so soaked in sweat already that no one could have known.

Then he understood that the other men were standing, that some had never dropped. Hennessey inspected his camera for grit; Nolan, trying to seem indifferent, reached for a canteen. A lieutenant came trotting down the road. "Fucking cherry," he said, and Nolan turned in alarm. But the lieutenant winked. "Fucking cherry. Shooting at a dead man!"

*   *   *

Down between the dunes a hundred fires were burning. Bodies lay in clumps like some substance that had dropped from the sky and melted, dotting the scorched grass. The grass held its form until a boot touched it and it disintegrated, smeared in the sand. Nolan kicked a dead man and leaped back from the flies—rising in a high whine, settling like a blanket. Something rustled in the thicket to his right.

A wounded man, he thought, and crouched. To the query in Hennessey's eyes Nolan shook his head, brought a finger to his lips. He crawled forward as Hennessey raised his camera, digging his rifle stock into the sand like a real soldier. He parted the brush.

A huge black man, naked, sat on a ruined parachute; a woman slept beside him. The man clasped his hands before his chest and rocked forward slightly, his eyes closed. Down his ribcage were moist red splotches of jungle rot, garish, unconvincing, like the makeup in a horror movie. The man didn't acknowledge Nolan but suddenly the woman's eyes opened.

"Excuse me," Nolan said.

18

"Scuse?"

He backed away, his eyes locked on the black man, who was still meditating. He stood and brushed at the sand.

"Dead or alive?" asked Hennessey.

He didn't know what to say. He began walking again, like a man entering upon some great natural wonder. The sun and drifting smoke, the bulldozers grunting by the sea, that charred helicopter, the endless confusion of wire twisting around the firebase—all seemed to whirl. A little flatbed truck pulled up behind him, loaded with dead; flies clung like paint. The driver was masked, his dull grey snout hanging like a baboon's nostrils, black hose crinkling round his neck; sweat streamed out of his hair and his forehead had erupted in a rash. He nodded hello. Could he possibly be smiling, this moon man? Someone praying in the bushes; someone smiling as he chauffeured the dead? Hennessey, who'd captured a nice panorama of the gleaming ocean, the island picturesque between the dunes, framed Nolan before the truck. "Smile."

"No, no. Don't man, not—"

"Your old lady'll love it. Smile." The camera whirred.

"You're crazy!" said Nolan. "You think I, you think I . . . what's wrong?"

Hennessey's face was white and wrenched. He jabbed his finger at the truck, but it was everywhere, like tear gas, like you'd been breathing through a tube and someone had pinched it off. Nolan felt his lungs heaving. Every man around him had picked up his feet. Oh, run!

*　　*　　*

"I'm really a pacifist," Nolan said, the words drifting out before him for study, like smoke rings. He was stoned, hard to say on what. He'd been talking to a soldier who didn't reply, but simply sat on the opposite bunk and strummed a guitar, in the dim light, like he wasn't there. There had been a crowd in the bunker but the rain stopped and they'd all gone off with Hennessey, speaking some foreign language, laughing.

"I mean, I almost went to Canada." The soldier gave a little flourish on his guitar, as though to underscore Nolan's stand for peace. "But I thought, I'd never see my parents again, or my girl. Do you have a girl?"

Nolan held out a picture, its edges curled from moisture, of his true love. The soldier kissed it like a cross. Then a grenade rolled across the floor.

There were raindrops on it; it sparkled. Nolan stared. He realized he was going to die. One, two, three, he counted, very calmly, and then leaped back on the bunk, jerked spasmodically. Four, five, six, he thought, staring up at the filament in the lightbulb.

The soldier kept playing his guitar. "That's just Fast-Man. Screws out the blasting cap, screws the top back on, pulls the ring. Damn nigger."

Here he was, beckoning. It was the man Nolan had met in the thicket; his eyes fled helplessly to the man's rotting skin, and he couldn't speak. Fast-Man turned and Nolan followed meekly to the roof of the bunker, where there was a sort of chaise longue, made of sandbags and flak jackets, all of it soaked. Wordlessly Nolan slid behind the machine gun. "When they lights up the sky, Nolan, you shoot this mother."

"You know my name!"

Fast-Man laughed. "I am Pie-in-the-Sky. I knows you like the back of my ass. I am your C of fucking O, cherry boy, Nolan babes."

"You're an officer? Sir?"

"I surely am, and this here is your on-the-job training. Are we ready on the right, are we ready on the left?" He lowered his voice, as though calling from a distance. "We is ready on the right, we is ready on the left. Aim that sucker!"

"There's nothing out there!"

Yet flares popped, lending the damp night luminescence. "You shoots at the rats, white boy. If you don't see no ghosts."

"Ghosts? You mean the gooks? Come back for their buddies?"

"Fire!" said Fast-Man, and the perimeter opened up, under the quaking light. Someone detonated a barrel of gasoline and there was a tower of red flame, crisscrossed with green tracers, Nolan's own. Nolan got under a rat and lifted it up into the concertina, where it hung until the gunner from the next bunker joined in, and cut it in two. "Fine, fine," Fast-Man said. "You good."

"I had an Expert rating in Basic."

"No shit? Well, drive on, Expert. See them ghosts?"

He did. Nolan could swear he saw them, men rising, men dancing, as round after round sank into the mass of bodies. The ghosts seemed to be brandishing rifles. He opened up.

"That's good," said Fast-Man. "You really good."

Nolan fired and fired again, hardly conscious of Fast-Man bending near, to fasten new clips. It was marvelous, how the shadows danced; he knew he hit them because of the lovely green tracers.

"Ceasefire!" Fast-Man yelled.

"Oh wow," said Nolan, leaning back in the chaise lounge.

"You all right, Nolan," Fast-Man said. "We gonna work you right into the program."

* * *

Nolan was sitting under the messtent. There was a steady breeze from the sea, and men bustled everywhere about him, with a sense of purpose in the morning's restorative air. Then the heat settled in and officers eyed him suspiciously. He glanced at his watch, brought out a tablet to write to his girl.

After half a dozen cups of coffee and four aspirins something hung on from the night still, blurred edges, a sort of after-image when he turned his head quickly. Two other soldiers waited as well; they didn't respond when Nolan smiled or even when he spoke: "You guys waiting for Fast-Man?" They talked in whispers if at all, with eye contact—intimate nods and murmurs, inexplicable quick laughter. One had a nasty cut up his cheek, bruised-looking along the stitches.

"Nolan, my man!"

There was relief, almost trust, in seeing Fast-Man again, here in this great pool of loneliness. Fast-Man grinned. Yet Nolan's eyes leaped to the camera hanging around Fast-Man's neck, and Fast-Man's grin changed to an expression of sympathy. "That man was your friend. Well, babes, I'm sorry. Though . . . he lucky."

"Hennessey . . . what? Was he hit?"

"One of them ghosts blowed away his kneecap. Million

21

dollar wound. Lucky . . . dudes was coming up to shake that man's hand. Went out in the night." Fast-Man grinned again. "Big bird come in, carried that man *away*."

Nolan glanced at the two men, who were standing up, nodding. "Fast-Man . . . the camera—"

"Been needing a good camera. 'Let me buy that from you, Mr. Million Dollars,' I told him. 'You be in Japan, they got everything there, dirt cheap.' Ever been to Japan, babes?"

"Changed planes. Fast-Man . . . wow. You know how I can write him? We went through Basic together."

"Sure, babes, come over to my house sometime, we take care of you. Fast-man never let you down, Nolan. Now. Look here. Time to go to work, babes."

The two men stood nearby.

"This here is your team, Nolan. This is Lewis—" Fast-Man nodded to the man with the cut; Nolan offered his hand, but Lewis drew back, almost imperceptibly, and merely smiled. "And this man is Sergeant Fisher." Fisher saluted with one finger. "Now these men are good men, Nolan. They know the score here in this combat area. You are in good hands with these men. Ain't no jiveassing with these men."

"Fast-Man, sir . . . about Hennessey. His old lady gave him that camera. I don't understand—"

"You gonna be just fine, Nolan babes," said Fast-Man. "Do what your team members say to do. New man, naturally, he gonna worry some. But I got faith in you, babes. Ain't no jiveassing with a man like you. Hey, babes. Keep your shit straight, do a good job for Fast-Man, your team members gonna find you a woman. Hey." He slapped Nolan on the back. "Like that, wouldn't you, babes?"

*　　*　　*

Fisher motioned to the pickup bed; before Nolan had found a grip he popped the clutch and was roaring out onto the road, into high, off across the smoldering plain and down along the beach. They passed the Australians, out surfing, sunning themselves. A big yellow-haired man flexed his biceps and waved.

Fisher hit the brakes and turned the pickup into a skid; Nolan

22

nearly went off the side. As he regained his balance Fisher slammed the truck into reverse and spun backward into a stand of scrub palms. Then he cut the motor. He opened the door but continued to sit, rolling a joint. Nolan came slowly around; Fisher struck a match on the dash. "So where you from in the World, cherry-boy?"

"Ohio. Van Wert, Ohio." Nolan stared at the joint, which Fisher passed to Lewis. Lewis got out and walked around to the front of the truck, where he smoked and looked out to sea. He pulled a frisbee from under his shirt and tossed it gently from hand to hand.

"They got any women in Van Wert?" Fisher asked. "I mean, Lewis and I were discussing it, you look queer to us."

Nolan took a step backward. Lewis was coming around the truck; he ran a finger along his cut, pulling at one of the stiches. "You guys are crazy," Nolan said.

"He thinks we're crazy," said Lewis, returning the joint to Fisher.

"Everybody here is crazy," Nolan said. "God, I wish I'd gone to Canada. I mean, I was going to." He sighed. "You guys aren't really like this, are you? You're just giving me shit."

"Oh, yes." Fisher smiled and released smoke. "We're plumb loco, no question about it. How it is, see, me and Lewis, we been under a strain."

"Tell you one thing," said Lewis. He jabbed Fisher's ribs and winked. "We're not crazy enough to throw them stinking gooks on the truck."

"I gotta do it by myself?"

" 'Fraid so," Fisher said. "How it is, see, me and Lewis got ourselves a union. We just drive. We're going up the beach now, and play with the girls, while you *load*." He stretched out his hand to Lewis, who had kept the joint too long. Lewis kept sucking; Fletcher gave him a little shove. "You get done, come see us."

"Got to work before you play," Lewis said, returning the joint at last. He began rolling another.

Nolan followed them for a few steps. "I won't do this alone!"

"Please," said Lewis.

"Do it for the team," said Fisher.

They went a distance down the beach, men the same height,

23

walking almost in step. They turned in unison.

"Masks are in the cab," Lewis called out.

"Real man don't need no mask," said Fisher. He was lighting the new joint. He'd taken off his boots and walked along in the water now. The two nodded, shrugged almost simultaneously, laughed. Lewis pulled out the frisbee again and Fisher ran out ahead, leaped high and gracefully, caught it.

*   *   *

Nolan sat on the tailgate, the sea lapping quietly in. He watched the fisherman pulling in their nets, out on the island. He found an overlooked stash in the cab and rolled himself a joint, then sat leafing through *Playboy*. He tried donning a mask, couldn't secure it, threw it aside. He rocked back and forth with the rhythm of the waves, then suddenly jerked to his feet and stumbled into the palms.

He dragged a body back by its heels. There were ants coming out of its mouth, and somehow an orange slime appeared on his shirt. He was surprised how little it weighed. He shoved it onto the bed and thought he could do this, could get through it, when his breakfast rose. He ran to the water and vomited. He looked up at last, blearily, his chest heaving. He could nearly make out the features of the men on the island, working so slowly, methodically, under the Buddha's eye. "Fast-Man, you prick," Nolan murmured.

Down the beach fifty meters the Australian was doing calisthenics. He waved, nodded in sympathy. "Oh . . . ain't it the shits, mate?"

"It's insane," said Nolan. "God Almighty, it's, it's—"

"It's the shits, mate."

Nolan sighed, stood weakly, shuffled toward the palms. He smoked another joint by the pickup door. Far up the beach, Lewis and Fisher were throwing the frisbee. The girls—on Hondas—were just now arriving. Okay, Nolan thought, I can do this, an initiation.

Here was a pile of men, hardly separable, like some odd shade of cheese shrunken by the sun. This one, take him: the side of his face, though waxen and greenish, seemed human still. Nolan turned him over, and the leathery flesh tore away . . .

24

Nolan's hands crawled with maggots. His skin was covered with slick little gleaming things . . . he brushed them against his thighs; they fell to his boot-tops. He swept at them frantically, stamped the sand, backed away . . . gagging in the violated air. The team wasn't looking. He leaned against the pickup, fighting for breath . . . even the Australian was gone. There he was, a few feet out, snorkeling. Oh Jesus, Lover of my Soul.

And . . . another four on the truck, by their boots. He could do this. He was a pacifist but he could do this . . . and then go for a Coke with the pretty ladies, and get stoned, and fuck. He'd be crazy enough by then. He tried not to look. He tried to send another self ahead to do the dirty work. He tried to hover above it all. He smoked another joint, and now, when he pulled out this new leg, and the bruised face rolled over, he thought it was Hennessey.

Of course not. If so, he certainly had some explaining to do. No, Hennessey was in Japan, shot while playing frisbee. With the same presence with which he'd counted off the dud grenade, Nolan saw that there was a trip wire tied to the dead man's neck, and that it stretched down to his hand, and because he'd turned the body over he'd yanked the pin from a grenade. As he counted, three, four, he wondered how the Australian could know. He was running: "Mate! Mate!" he cried. "Boobytrap!" Trap for boobies. Nolan threw his hands before his face, and leaped back.

*   *   *

The moon hung low over the sea, impossibly large, red. He'd been lying among the dead, and quickly, horrified, he rose and ran down the beach. He knelt and washed his hands, his face. They had abandoned him!

He was angry, yet afraid. Lunatics. The firebase was brightly-lit, and he walked toward it, light-headed, thirsty. The air was cold. He detoured the dead but began running toward the light, any light . . . a flare popped directly above him. He was standing by more dead men, pulled up together. More flares, and he waved his rifle frantically, jumped up and down, shouted.

He heard the faint call: "Fire!"

Then the night was all flame and noise; bullets dug up the sand around him and strafed the dead men. They thought he was a gook! He dropped to the sand, crawled, curled in among the dead.

"Follow me, Nolan."

A huge black man, his chest gleaming from wounds, stood in the half-light by the sea.

"Fast-Man! Is it you? Fast-Man, this is a mistake, I—"

The flares began winking out. "Ceasefire!" echoed faintly. Nolan ran after the black man, along the beach. "Fast-Man!" he called, but no one answered. No answer, no sound but the water, and a subtle rustling, no more than wind, as dark men came in waves off the field, and entered the water. Once more he heard his name, and seemed to see Fast-Man's head rolling over and over.

He was imagining this. He was in the middle of a dream, and would awaken in Japan, in a hospital, screaming. Yet still he entered the water, and swam toward the island, the dim yellow Buddha. Salt burned at the hole in his stomach but he found he could swim almost effortlessly.

Tanks

The tanks were pulled into a circle with their howitzers pointed out, as though Indians were expected. Around the circle was a field of grass taller than a man but uniform as any wheatfield, rolling out almost a kilometer to the jungle wall. The jungle hulked over the grass in a long curve to the horizon, and you couldn't see into it. It seemed more black than green, a wet cold place that Porter was glad to be even this far removed from. Behind the jungle was an orange glow, and surely that would be the sun, the one that had already been to Missouri.

Porter had awakened shivering, his bedroll crested with dew, his neck aching. The dawn was clear but he knew it would rain, as it had yesterday and the day before. He lay watching Okie, wishing he might return to dreams; Okie was standing by the inside track of the point team's Sheridan, looking out. "Morning," he said, nodding, holding out a handful of red clay. "Look at this, Porter. Man could farm this. Just like Oklahoma."

"Not dry enough." Porter buttoned his shirt and pulled on his boots, threw his poncho liner atop the tank to dry. He picked up his rifle from where his bed had been and propped it across his pack, barrel down. "Christ, it's cold."

"It'll warm up, troop."

He followed Okie toward the chowline, massaging his neck and wondering if he could get by another day without shaving. Maybe, unless there was no mission and they stayed here another day and night, in which case Lieutenant Wolfe would make everyone shave in the interest of morale. Morale wasn't so much low as hungover, Porter thought: every evening there was a party until two. He himself was on the wagon: just sixty-four days to go.

He rolled his neck and stretched his arms toward the sky. Oh dear God it was a beautiful morning, even if he'd been standing on the moon. If a man could wake up somewhere, and not have a thing to do . . . meet Chris for lunch, take in a movie to beat the heat. A smell hit him like a dream. "They got bacon!"

"I guess," said Okie. They were far back in the line. "I cain't see nothing but that fucking grapefruit juice."

"You mean that powdered stuff they mix up? Like Tang?"

"Tang in the flesh, troop."

"The astronauts drink that for breakfast."

"There it is. We gonna fly away, oh glory."

"I wish."

The tank commander broke through the line between them, his plate heaped high with bacon and some of the eggs that had somehow survived yesterday's long ride. Porter reeled slightly, expecting a ritual glare at least, or even to be thrown out of the line for his whiskers. The commander passed without so much as raising his eyes.

"Asshole," Okie said.

"What the hell." Porter shrugged. "At least they feed us good."

In the month since they'd been attached to armored the commander had not been seen to speak to any of the infantry except Captain Diemer, who rode along atop the commander's tank, like some captured chief. Diemer was a tall, grave man, a West Pointer who took every wound and death personally; the commander was short and nearly bald and—his own men said—had barely made it through OCS. He'd been dragged screaming from some sleepy little fort down in Texas, across the wide and forgetful sea. Ah, but status! The armored had it; nothing was lower than infantry.

Attaching them to armored had been Jolly Green's—the Colonel's—idea: more firepower, more kills. He flew over every day, like a businessman checking on his investment. He seldom landed, instead calling down the coordinates of where the enemy was likely to be; sometimes he flew ahead of them, a guidon, a god on a horse. Toward lunch he'd drop low, swoop back over them, and bank off into the sun.

So far they'd done little but burn gasoline. The infantry, needing camouflage to be whole, rode high for all to see, clutching at gear, hanging on. The rain scratched their eyes and the steel plate bruised their bones until, like so many RV's in a caravan, they parked in another broad field. As long as they avoided contact, Porter was content, but he understood how Okie or Lieutenant Wolfe could feel superfluous. Rifles and tripflares and even mines were ridiculous things, alongside the defenses a tank could muster. The enemy would have needed to be both crazy and high to come charging across an open field, into howitzers and .50 caliber machine guns.

The infantry was used to silence, and all the shouting, the great engines revving, helicopters coming and going, seemed sacriligious. After dark radios blasted away—enough to frighten away the Devil himself, let alone any little green men. If Porter stepped outside the perimeter, to urinate, a circle of noise and light would seem to be throbbing like one great generator, forgotten in the wasteland. It was a landing of aliens; soon every city would be doomed. Black men danced, moaned in communion, shook fists at the moon. Good old boys strummed battered PX guitars and sang about no-good women. A Texan who had played for Buck Owens held the stage for a time, but finally the Rear Action Trash heard about him, kidnapped him to play for officers down in Saigon.

With his breakfast finished, a second cup of coffee in hand, Porter began writing a letter to Trudy, a girl from his mother's church. He'd dated her several times, the summer before he was drafted. That was also the summer his true love Chris hitchhiked to Seattle, flowers in her hair. Trudy was definitely second-best, but at least she was there.

Apparently Trudy and Porter's mother had had a talk. Her letters had begun arriving regularly, in colored envelopes, on delicate, heavily-perfumed paper. Often the letters infuriated him: she actually spoke of how fascinating his father's business was, the parts business, genuine NAPA parts. This morning he found himself proposing. "Dearest Trudy, if I make it through this, I want you to know that—" He stopped. What would she do? He feared she'd accept. Rather a costly way to prove he existed. No . . . good Lord, no.

Perhaps it was that writing to a hometown girl was too much like the movies. Trudy would receive his proposal and answer frantically, "Yes! Yes! Yes!"—except that, poor bastard, he'd been captured by the moon men. Unspeakable atrocities: bamboo slivers under his fingernails, made to drink urine. Cut to Trudy as played by Rita Hayworth, crying late into the night, faithful to his sacrifice, transported by their perfect love, beyond that seemingly final telegram: "Missing in Action." Later, pressed by her poverty and an unscrupulous employer, she *would* marry, not realizing that at that very moment Porter, played by Errol Flynn, was staggering from the jungle, having singlehandedly restored democratic safeguards to the quaint little republic of Laos.

It was hot now. He crumpled his letter and threw it aside. He opened a can of apricots and chugged the syrup. "Hear about sergeant yet, Okie?"

There was a vacancy: Lieutenant Wolfe had joined them, and their platoon sergeant had left, almost three months before. Okie was a logical choice, and so was Snowball, the machine-gunner—at least when he wasn't stoned.

"It ain't come through yet," Okie said. He slid the bolt of his rifle back and forward, spread a drop of oil with his finger. "I asked Wolfe, but he put me off."

"That's his style. Lead you on, let you down. You'll get it. They *got* to give it to you."

"Yeah."

Porter lay against his pack. Nothing could happen until Jolly Green flew over; a lot of the men were nodding back to sleep, before the sun grew too merciless. His eyes fell to Snowball, who was sitting atop the gun team's tank twenty meters away.

Snowball waved awkwardly: he and Porter hadn't spoken for days. This when, months like years before, they'd been best of friends. Something had gone awry when they'd left for R. & R. Porter had tried to talk Snowball into going to Australia, but while they awaited their flight Snowball began hanging out with the brothers—jive-ass niggers, Okie would have called them. Anyhow it was a group Porter couldn't join. He left for white man's country, while Snowball went to Bangkok; Snowball returned with the clap, and Porter with the notion he might marry Trudy.

Snowball was talking to Dover, a black man, and several of the black armored. Wasn't it a private party? Only Billy Boy—new in-country, reminiscent to Porter of himself somehow—seemed to belong, blue eyes and all. Billy Boy smoked dope recklessly, even in daytime, even on patrols. Now, atop the tank, he pirouetted to the music, hands fluttering in imitation of something vaguely feminine. The blacks, shirts off, sitting cross-legged or prone to sun themselves, clapped for Billy Boy, who at last stumbled and plopped heavily beside his buddy Dover.

These days Porter kept company, pulled guard, with Okie and Preacher. There were some new men in the platoon, whose names he hadn't learned; he didn't want to know them. Occasionally he'd turn his head to see one of them staring at him, in a mixed awe and challenge. This shocked him, to realize that he was seen as the old pro—a true alien, with only a murky sense of what the World had been.

"Good morning, Preacher," Porter said. Preacher nodded, tried to smile. He had finished breakfast and was having devotions. Lately he pursued the perfection of his soul with a frenzy, reading his New Testament, kneeling to pray when the sun had gone down and the marijuana smoke filled the air and the men sang and danced in what must have seemed to Preacher like the cacophany of hell. Preacher's eyes had an intensity, and his face had taken on a pallor, that made men avoid him. Perhaps it was God's wrath they feared. Not so long ago, before they had joined the armored, Cherokee platoon had blown up three North Vietnamese coming down a trail—spooks in the night, suddenly lit up by a tripflare and the explosion of Claymores, light like a camera's flash. Dried fish rained in the camp, and Preacher went balmy, screaming soon that Jesus would return. As if to confirm his prophecy, lightning quaked on the horizon, lending a yellow outline to dark clouds. Lieutenant Wolfe had to scream at him, even strike him, before Preacher understood how dangerous his antics were. Ever since, his eyes had had a wounded look.

He began now, yet once again, to witness to Porter. Porter nodded absently: He'd grown up with it, and didn't mind. He was calculating how much time he had left: drop ten days for a leave, another ten to process out, only forty-three days. How to speed it up, dream it away? Preacher's talk, with all the emotion of an altar call, reminded him of Trudy, who wrote so faithfully, and then too of Chris, who had never written. If the subject were religion then he thought that the loyalty of Christian women was wonderful; why was it that Chris had proved so unloyal? Why couldn't you have the loyalty of one, the intelligence of the other? Not that Trudy was stupid, but ... "Yes, yes," he said, responding to some craziness of Preacher's. Preacher must have concluded that the moment for Porter's redemption had finally arrived, for now he went on more intensely, even stammering in his eagerness, not saying that it was likely to rain or that he hoped for word today from that amazingly loyal woman, his wife. It was as though he were trying to dynamite Porter into salvation: "Are you an atheist?"

Heavy artillery. The saved of his mother's church invoked it on special occasions, because it was hard to conceive of anyone so decadent as to answer, "Yes," while an uneasy "Well, no . . ." might bring the opportunity to kneel, confess all. "No," Porter said quickly, "I'm a Democrat." Okie laughed aloud, but Preacher looked as though he'd been shot, and immediately Porter was sorry. Still, he couldn't manage to say anything further to Preacher, and the three of them fell silent. Having tried to postpone it, Porter lit his first Pall Mall. Then he lit another. He thought of a place on the Gasconade River where he used to fish: crappie, white bass. And then he was lifting his head slowly to a shout, a clanking, as though he'd fallen into a dream.

He saw a crane. It was huge, with a white neck; except for the black tips of its wide wings, it was white. With the early sun, the damp-looking jungle, it suggested a cool pastoral; its wings seemed to sweep in time with the rolling grass. It flew low, ponderously, alien to the aliens, correct. "Caree . . . Caree . . . " it sang.

It crossed the sun, and the sun, too, was correct: wild and orange and over-sized, holding the crane. There had been such moments in Missouri, on land so backward Porter thought he was the first to come calling. Once he'd surprised a hawk, stood back frightened as it shot away, and he thought, I'm not needed here.

"Jesus," said Okie, softly. The three of them had stood to watch the crane. Then the dream was over: Billy Boy raised his rifle, thumbed it to automatic, let fly six rounds.

Porter was amazed. Of course! If you had a gun you could shoot it. It hadn't occurred to him. Stunned, he nodded stupidly as Preacher stepped forward, raised a hand like a prophet, and shouted, "Don't shoot that bird!"

But all the perimeter had the idea. Men leaped up on the tanks and wheeled the .50 Calibers around. The morning roared alive. The crane flew past the sun, seemed to hang in the air before a dead tree, the only one on the plain. Then it fell. Officers ran up, to protest the firing, but it had already ceased.

*   *   *

Porter and Okie sat in the shadow of their Sheridan, sipping iced grapefruit juice. Preacher was asleep, his mouth open and his glasses askew; his forehead glistened. All was quiet.

Across the perimeter, Lieutenant Wolfe stood to stretch periodically, as though to put some idea in motion, but then he'd look at the sky and sit again. Jolly Green still hadn't arrived, which was unusual, poising the day between dread and hope. Dread of a bad mission; hope for another twenty-four hours without risk. Maybe he'd get a hot lunch today, Porter thought, a siesta, even a shower under that blimp hoisted up by the wrecker track. Maybe there would be a letter from Trudy.

"You like Ann Margret?" Okie asked.

"Huh?" Porter had been dozing. "Sure."

"I been sitting here thinking. They oughtta fix it up, you get back to the World, you can have any movie star you want."

"What's in it for her?"

Okie nodded. "Nothing much."

"Wouldn't be any fun. Those movie stars are miserable."

"The hell. All that money? Wild parties?"

"Take it from me, man: Ann-Margret's miserable."

"How the fuck do you know?"

"I'm psychic."

Dover was crossing to Wolfe's position from the gun team tank; huge grasshoppers leaped before him in the smashed-down grass. His uniform was clean, and his cheeks, a damp brown, were smoothly shaven. He was carrying all of his gear. He reached Wolfe and turned his back, propping up his pack on the end of his rifle barrel. In a moment Wolfe shook his head angrily.

"What's going on?" Porter asked.

"Oh, he's trying to get out early on his R. & R."

"Good luck."

"He ain't so much as said hello to me in three weeks, then he comes over this morning, while you and Preacher was still sleeping, and wants me to talk to Wolfe. He says his little gal

33

friend got her signals crossed, and she's already in Honolulu. I said T.S., brother. Wolfe won't go for that. He ain't that stupid."

"Hell, even I could have come up with a better story."

"Naw, it's the truth. He showed me her letter. But man, you know as well as I do that the Army don't make no accommodations. That gal can fucking wait. What pisses me off, he's got the nerve, you know? It ain't just that he's black as sin. Snowball wouldna done that."

Porter sighed. "Snow's kinda strange lately . . ."

"There it is. Got a bone up his ass, I don't know what's come over him. Thinks he's a fucking leader of men. But listen to me, now, speaking a Dover. You're a pretty level-headed troop, I'm gonna ask you something."

"Me? I'm just a stupid grunt, man."

"Don't fuck with it. You're alive, ain't you? No shame in being infantry. I'm asking you, what you think, bout Dover and this little white girl?"

"Aw . . . Okie. Maybe she's big, man. Maybe she's six foot two."

"You . . . I just think, you know, I think they's two races, I don't care what you say."

"Don't get off on this, man."

"You take, where my daddy used to work, they was this old colored man, sweet old man. Only along come the N. double-A. C. P., and you cain't even talk to him."

At college Porter had cut classes with Chris to attend anti-war rallies; the strength of his convictions had had a lot to do with the brand-new marvels of sex. Left over in the revolutionary air had been the black cause. Some bragged they'd actually been on the march to Selma, a distinction very nearly as powerful as having seen the Beatles in concert. Anyhow Porter had prided himself on being color-blind. Though he was a backslid liberal now, as he had been a backslid Christian and would become, if his luck held, a backslid killer, there were still times when he thought of himself as . . . well, an intellectual. Wasn't he in this mistaken war by mistake? Okie's talk was something like a violation of his carefully enshrined memories of Chris. "Man, you can't go around saying stuff like that. Stuff like that, I mean, it's all settled. Dover's fine when the shit flies. Huh?"

Okie pointed triumphantly. "Look there, I told you Wolfe

wasn't that stupid."

Apparently not: Wolfe rose quickly and strode away from Dover, shaking his head. And, Jolly Green or no Jolly Green, he appeared to have reached a decision about something else, as well, something more than a directive to shave, Porter guessed. He felt a mild °panic, thinking that he might somehow be affected. No. He'd been a good boy lately, straight enough for promotion. Wasn't he already a point man, the worst thing you could be? Still . . . one of Wolfe's oddities was how he sized you up. When Wolfe joined them he'd somehow concluded that Porter was the best point man he had; nothing less than a bullet could change his mind. Porter had begged for a clerk's job in the rear, to carry ammo behind Snowball—even to take the radio. No dice.

Wolfe motioned to Porter and Okie, to the gun team and second squad. Porter picked up Preacher's glasses from where they had fallen in the grass, shook him awake. Preacher sat up, blinked; "Oh," he said, softly. Porter handed him the glasses. "It's powwow time."

"Should I bring the radio?"

"No, no. You won't need it. Something's up, though."

They walked across the perimeter, the heat hanging down on their clothing. Porter batted at grasshoppers with an open hand. Preacher slouched along behind them, and they stopped to wait.

"How many days you got?" Okie asked.

"Sixty-three and a wake-up. Short."

"Christ. That ain't short."

"I'm shorter than a copperhead snake, fucker."

"I'll be back on the block smoking see-gars fore you make it to Tay Ninh."

"Shit, Okie, you're gonna re-up. You know you're a lifer. What you got to go home for, besides that old broken-down Cream-O?"

"Camaro, troop. And watch your mouth. That car is some very hot poop."

"Bet your old lady throws a rod."

"She does, and I'll—"

Lieutenant Wolfe was shaking his head, motioning them away. Porter looked up.

Here came Jolly Green.

*   *   *

35

On the near horizon, his bird seemed to pierce the waves of heat, and drop instantly out of the high cold air. It thundered down the field, flying low and fast, echoing off the jungle. It veered left and right, dipped up its nose, and sped in—all very theatrical, as if under attack. Still, when the bird hovered, it had a lovely arrogance, like an old Lincoln, perhaps, a machine gone beyond its makers into its own identity. It touched the ground without a jolt, in time with the earth's subtle motion. The pilot, no more than a silhouette behind the glare of the windshield, flipped back his helmet, sat smoking. He throttled low, idled, and revved up again, like a kid at a stoplight.

Porter glanced toward Lieutenant Wolfe, whose cheeks were jerking involuntarily. Had he wanted to be a warrant officer, to make daring rescues, be weighted down with medals and wounds? Nothing, Porter thought, was lower than infantry. Beside Wolfe, Dover had stepped back, disgust large in his face; he dropped his pack to the ground.

Jolly Green had stepped from the bird as it touched down, he also in time with the earth. It was as though he had simply materialized, like Captain Kirk himself. For him to stumble would have been inconceivable. He barely bent his head beneath the rotor blades, and magically his cap stayed on. Not Captain Kirk: he was immaculate, cool, like a game show host. Captain Diemer and the tank commander ran up under the wind, crouched like refugees.

Jolly Green towered over them, wrung their hands, threw an arm around each. Such a big man! He walked them round and round the bird—and they followed like children who had been on their own and done well but now were reminded of their true worth, before their angry and purposeful father. Jolly Green produced a map, brandished a grease pencil: they took out their own maps, nodded solemnly. He pointed down the field in the direction from which he had come, made complicated motions with his hands. There was a question from Diemer—shouted, but inaudible—and another from the commander. Jolly Green shook his head impatiently, then nodded with approval.

"What the fuck," Okie said.

Now Jolly Green shook hands and jerked away toward the command bird; left so suddenly behind, out of time, the two officers looked shabby and inadequate. Inside his bird, Jolly

Green held up a thumb, then looked straight ahead; it was as though he had already left the earth. The pilot had been revving the engine, and when the thumb rose he ripped away at what seemed almost full speed. The wind blew the grass flat, and paper plates left over from breakfast sailed across the field.

Unconsciously Porter took a step forward, into the vacuum left by the bird. Air seemed to rush past him. With all the others, he lifted his head toward the sky. He lifted his rifle, and it occurred to him that if a crane could be shot from the sky, so could a helicopter. How pretty to see it drop like a spear! To see it tear to pieces where the jungle began, see the core of fire burn white-hot after the explosion, black smoke rolling over the wreckage, foliage wilting. And to see the titans running into the grass, themselves afire . . . Jolly Green banked off toward the sun, climbing.

*   *   *

"Two things," said the Lieutenant. He moved his hands in precise ways, forcefully but as though in imitation of something, like a basketball coach Porter had had once. "First, at 0600 hours this morning, a Chinook cargo ship passed over this grid . . . " He slashed at a point on his map with a grease pencil. " . . . about ten kilometers from here. The Chinook monitored a strong radio signal."

Wolfe paused to seek eye contact. The movies again, Porter thought: they nestled inside everyone. He, too, had yearnings to make a grand speech, at a pivotal moment. Was all of this so important?

He was standing behind Snowball. Moments before, Snowball had slapped him on the back and said, "Hey babes, how come you don't come see me no more? We be lonely."

"Yeah. Aw . . . Snow, I—"

"Come on over tonight, babes. We get fucked up good. Short-timers, right?"

"Right." And maybe he would join that group again, get stoned, float away with Hendrix and James Brown. Maybe; he turned his head from Snowball's broad back to watch Okie, who was chewing gum and nodding emphatically, as though he already had been informed of what Wolfe was saying.

"The signal might have come from a relay transmitter to the North—no sweat. Probably wouldn't be anybody there. But Battalion thinks it could be that regimental headquarters you've all heard about, and I think you know what that means. Boocoo Charley. A regular shitload of gooks."

This brought questions, ritual protests, but Wolfe shook his head. His face shifted, and he seemed to apologize. "I don't know any more, men. Nobody does. Except that we're moving out in ten minutes." He dropped his voice, like Porter's coach again, before the game: "Get—your shit— together." Porter thought he detected a flash of doubt in the man's eyes. Genuine worry? So many times Battalion had hyped things up, and only a long hot ride resulted.

Everyone was talking—angrily, bitterly, fearfully, but there was also a kind of cautious enthusiasm in the air, a rising energy. Hearing "ten minutes," some had begun to move away, only to stop; Wolfe had also said, "two things." Porter hadn't moved. Wolfe had his attention now. The man seemed upset, and there had been other moments like this one, when after great delibera-tion he arrived at a decision no one could have predicted, a course of action that was almost intellectual. Don't be afraid, Porter told himself. And here at last it was, Wolfe's little masterpiece of bad timing. Like the dead crane, it was what was wrong with the day. Wolfe took a cheery, camp counselor's tone:

"The second thing is, I've decided to make Snowball my platoon sergeant. I've put him in for stripes."

At first there was no reaction. Men in second squad moved away when there was no further restraint from Wolfe; this would affect them very little. The newer men in first squad looked serious, but were silent; possibly they didn't understand. Dover seemed agitated, but more than likely it was because his plan to leave had taken a further setback; that would mean more to him than a brother's promotion or Okie's humiliation. Only Billy Boy's reaction was positive. He broke into a brief applause, which, in its isolation, gave the moment an odd turn. Then, after the first wave of surprise, and a sort of awe, had passed over his face, Okie flicked his eyes from Wolfe to Snowball—perhaps searching for collusion. Snowball licked his lips but was also silent, passing down, Porter thought, into some deep and incoherent state, yet with something rising in him simultaneously, some ghost.

"This is no reflection on you, Okie," Wolfe said, in a tone that reached for intimacy and warmth, before the quickly dwindling group of men. "In the time I've known you I've been impressed with your leadership potential. And really, really, who can say? Maybe I'm all wrong here, but we've had that vacancy for too long, and it seemed to me that Snowball, at this point in time, was the best man for the job."

Porter moved the best he could to calm things. He slapped Snowball on the back, overcoming the slight revulsion he always felt for another man's sweat. "Congratulations."

Snowball stared at him sadly, yet with a new face; lifting his chin, he seemed suddenly fiercer, like a recruitment poster. "Thank you, sir," he said.

"You'll work for it," Wolfe said.

"Fucking lifers," Okie said. Wolfe ignored him, like a teacher who owed one favor to his class, and had granted it.

"Dover take my gun?" Snowball asked.

"Right," said Wolfe, assurance returning to his voice. "All right, all right, let's move!"

He didn't understand, Porter thought. That was what was wrong with him. Wolfe didn't understand what his words could do, so that his little dramas were more unnerving than triumphant. First squad moved, but slowly, grievingly. Everyone liked Snowball. Even so it all was wrong, too quick, too late. Information was faulty. Abilities were inadequate. Dear God, stop it, Porter thought. Let me off.

"Sir?" Dover said, hanging back.

"What? What?"

"Sir, I have to get out. My old lady—"

"What is it with you, troop? We got a *combat mission!*"

Dover nodded and trotted off, but his head was bent, masking rage. Wolfe glared at Porter and Preacher, and they backed away, amazed. Okie walked ahead of them, arms swinging wildly.

"Is it gonna be bad, Porter?" Preacher asked.

"I don't know. Take it slow. Watch yourself."

"I'll stay by you."

"Okay."

They hurried to scoop up gear, chug sodas, push rounds into

chambers, grab grenades. They crawled atop the Sheridan; the driver, deep below, had started the engine and wheeled the turret around forward. A soldier from another tank ran up, jumped high, and retrieved his shirt from where it had been hanging on the howitzer barrel. Porter squatted, not yet courageous enough to sit directly on the steel. Heat from the engine ebbed up.

"Fucking lifers," said Okie, almost crying.

*   *   *

Their destination was a numbered patch of green, a rectangular slice of jungle twenty kilometers long and twelve wide, nestled against Cambodia. There was no village, no farmland, nothing; when the tanks had changed direction several times, Porter could not even have told which way was Tay Ninh. He scooted carefully, on the moving tank, to sit on his pack. It was cooler.

They'd make a fine target for mortars, he thought, as the two files of tanks merged, and rolled down an isthmus of grass connecting two fields. The jungle met above them, and a troupe of monkeys fled across the meshed sky, back into bamboo. But there were no mortars. Porter shifted hands on his grab bar, wiped off the sweat, studied the new woodlines.

They halted on the long side of the rectangle and Cherokee platoon dismounted. They dropped into the grass as though into a pool, bobbed up, tried to group amid all the noise. There was a splash, a curse, someone laughing. Then they were zigzagging toward the woods, a zombie-like procession of floating heads. They gathered at the jungle's edge, which was tall old trees here, unscathed by artillery and with no brush beneath, a park.

The theory was that the North Vietnamese, assuming there were any, would run from the advance of the tanks and the remaining infantry, into Cherokee's ambush. Cherokee's was the safer assignment, since they wouldn't need to expose themselves, could burrow down, stick their rifles in front of their faces. Nonetheless it seemed to Porter like the main body was deserting them. When Cherokee had threaded into the trees, and the tanks were rolling again, Porter watched Preacher. Preacher had the

40

handset cupped to his ear. His face would change should Cherokee run into an ambush before it could construct one.

In another twenty minutes the tanks had reached their entry point on the short side of the rectangle. They lined up parallel, fifteen meters apart, fifty meters from the jungle wall. Down the line Porter could see Captain Diemer and then Wolfe waving, and the infantry dropped into the grass, trying to land solidly. Snowball waded the grass between first squad's point and gun teams, yelling at the new men, "Behind the tanks!" He grinned at Porter, as if to demonstrate that such mundane advice was not meant for him. Porter threw him a mock salute, already too weary to attempt a shout above the engines. Snowball turned sharply, his face fluid, as though the salute has truly been mockery. He moved toward Wolfe's tank.

Porter stumbled behind the Sheridan and knelt, not wanting to present a target before he had to, even if it were merely flashes of his head and shoulders. The ground was moist but the long shoots of grass dry and brittle; he couldn't breathe, and stood again. The engines had throttled low, awaiting word from Cherokee. Porter pointed to the radio, but Preacher shook his head. Porter removed his helmet, dropped his pack, and searched for more Pall Malls.

Smoking absently, he watched the gunner atop the demolition track, twenty meters away. The man stood and ripped off his helmet. That would break his radio contact with the other vehicles, a minor taboo. But now he was simply a man, with shaggy hair and a ragged tee shirt, rather than a connection in a weapon in a long circuit of weapons, jerking and firing when whispers were in his ear. He stretched and scratched his chest, as though to say, "There. We got here, at least." He lit a cigarette, passed it down to the hand of the driver, reaching up from inside. He took it back, said something, waited, nodded, smiled. Then he fell forward, looking puzzled. He struck his knee on a bolt head, and his face, with a quick pain, grew blank.

He was dead. So many engines were running that no one had heard the shot. Nonetheless every gunner tensed, hugged his weapon; surely ears were buzzing. When down the line the commander nodded, all the .50 calibers opened up, slicing down the bamboo that began the jungle here. It dropped delicately, sifting to the ground along with tall weeds and grass, as though with so many rounds it was momentarily suspended. The firing was vengeful, more sustained and disciplined than the firing at the crane had been. It was pride, and nothing could withstand it.

When it had ceased Porter could see Diemer talking on the Battalion radio, and shortly artillery was whistling in from the firebase. Fire flared wherever grass had been when the rounds exploded, and smoke hung in layers beneath the jungle canopy. Deeper within, trees cracked and toppled.

Medics had picked up the dead man and were carrying him through the grass to a place further behind. The grass whipped round them: if fire caught it, everything would jump up in a quick terror. A detail sliced grass with machetes, to establish an Aid Station, and the medical track withdrew. Porter turned his eyes.

Word came that Cherokee had established its ambush. Two Sheridans, neither of them Porter's, rumbled forward for the point, and the other tanks moved laboriously into files behind them. Snowball spread his men out between the files. Porter concentrated on his footing.

There was a deeper rumble, like an unexpected chord in a piece of music. Porter saw lightning. He looked up and the rain was falling gently, the sun reflected in it still; he realized he hadn't lifted his head to the sky in several hours. The rain could become a problem, but for now it cooled him, offered a brief serenity. The tanks themselves steamed and seemed to run more quietly, as though they were drinking rain.

The tanks leaned up against, and then uprooted, trees six inches in diameter. The bamboo splintered and fell like wheat before combines. It became a mat of arched branches, and shortly this was wet: Porter fell, ripped his pants at the knee.

Smoking another Pall Mall, he stared ahead into a jungle that with the rain had grown darker, more deceptive. He could see Captain Diemer, atop the command tank, speaking into a handset carried, now, by someone Porter didn't know. The black man Johnson, the Captain's radio man before this one, had long since left for a supply job in Tay Ninh: a bed to sleep in, good food, whores. Most important, he was certain to make it home. Porter had lobbied hard for Johnson's job, but Wolfe had blocked it, with the deluded notion that Porter was a born point man, that pointing was his destiny. Porter understood that he'd never have

42

a rear job. He barely knew Captain Diemer. He was where he'd started: nothing much learned, near to death as ever. Just now it didn't matter. Black or white, soon they'd all be equal.

*   *   *

There was sporadic small arms fire a long way ahead. Porter glanced toward Preacher, who was near Snowball because of the radio; they stood in a mist of exhaust. Preacher nodded. "They're running into Cherokee."

"Maybe we won't have to go all the way in," a new man said.

"No way," Okie said, moving up.

Snowball danced about, trying to keep the squad apart should mortars begin; he walked back to confer with Wolfe, who was managing second squad. Dover and Billy Boy stood a distance from everyone else. Dover talked earnestly; Billy Boy giggled.

Heavy fire opened up on the right. From behind a shield, his body half out of the tube that plunged into the machine itself, the gunner atop the right point tank returned the fire, until his barrel steamed. Grenades went out; smoke drifted back and clung like fog. The gunner resumed his firing. Wolfe ordered the platoon out to the flank, and Porter crouched, trying to see something to aim at.

Now the gunner in the tube fired with one hand, his free arm twisting in the air, like a rodeo rider's. His tank wheeled beneath him to advance; there was a deep muffled explosion, and a clot of smoke, as the tank hit a mine. Part of a tread flew back and landed behind first squad. One side of the tank lifted off the ground, and when it fell again the gunner was bucked up into the air. He came down dead, slumped in his seat. A rocket sailed in and exploded below his neck; the head and chest disappeared.

Firing from the nearby tanks stopped abruptly, with men shouting, the smoke everywhere. Diemer stood, far up in the right column, and screamed that a jet was coming in. Porter crawled backward, gingerly on the bamboo, marveling that anyone would stand up in the middle of a firefight. He reached for another Pall Mall, but the pack was wet: no time to dig within his gear.

43

"Man hurt!" Billy Boy was shouting. "Man hurt!"

There were two neat small holes at Dover's wrist. Beside him, Billy Boy poked into the bamboo with his rifle barrel, and looked grim. Snowball and Wolfe came quickly.

"Let's see," said Wolfe. He glanced around him, at the rest of the squad. "Don't bunch up!"

"Fuck," said Okie. "He ain't hurt. It's just—"

Billy Boy brushed past, knelt, propped Dover up. "You gonna be all right, Dove?"

"Oh wow . . . " Dover said, faintly. "It hurts."

"Sure it does, Dove."

"Jesus Fucking Christ," Okie said. "He done that himself. Lieutenant, you cain't—"

"Well, I *saw* it," Billy Boy said, indignantly, pointing down at the bamboo. "I saw it."

"Snake," murmured Porter, only now understanding.

"Maybe it wasn't poisonous," Wolfe said hopefully. He shook his head and looked anxiously toward Diemer, then Snowball. He opened his mouth to speak, but had to pause as the jet made its first attack, dropping two five hundred pounders with a clunk and fiery crashing. Debris settled with the rain. "What do you think, Snow?" Wolfe asked, though still his voice, the entire matter, was at odds with a burst of AK-47 fire that began before the jet was quite up the sky again.

"Wasn't no snake at all," Okie insisted.

"You don't know. You can't be sure, babes," said Snowball. He knelt. "You shamming it, Dove?"

"Lord . . . " Dover moaned. "Please, please . . . "

Okie turned angrily away. Wolfe stepped past Dover, moving toward Captain Diemer, who had motioned from atop the command tank. "I—don't— know," Wolfe said, his voice cut up again by small arms, like a bad radio transmission. "We have to let him go. Dover, if you . . . Yes. We'll let him go. Get two of the new men, Snow; they can carry him back to the field." Wolfe frowned. There was a momentary lull in the firing, and he sounded decisive. "Move it! Break it up here. Spread out!"

"You'll be okay, Dove," said Billy Boy.

". . . Shit," said Dover, shivering as though in withdrawal.

The jet pounced again, strafing; the empty shell casings pattered through the leaves overhead, like little bombs. Porter stood beside Okie. They watched until the jet had veered up again. Two men—straining to conceal their delight—were carrying Dover away.

"I'd a fixed his black ass," Okie said. "I'd put him on the point, see how he liked that. You hear Snow? Those bastards stick together. Just because he cain't wait to go on R. & R. like anybody else. You don't catch the point team pulling that shit."

Porter shrugged. "Beats me, man. Some guys are smarter than we are."

Okie bent and held his hand near the bamboo. "Snake," he said. "Nice snake. Here, snake."

*　　*　　*

Porter glimpsed the belly of Jolly Green's bird, a dull green above the treetops, its landing lights flashing. More AK fire, and the bird lifted sharply from sight, high into the rain.

A burst of machine gun fire ripped across the demolition track. Soon the crew was leaping off, and smoke poured from within. Coils of white detonator cord leaped up, extended, snapped in the air like electric arcs. A man still on top was blown to the ground, and hunched along painfully, his shirt quickly soaking in blood. Rocking with explosions, puffs of smoke rising from every opening, the track plowed off into the bamboo, stalled, died, sprouted flame.

Ahead, the disabled point tank looked like some blinded green beast as the driver tried to maneuver out of the way of the columns behind him, only to hit another mine. Steam hissed, and a fountain of coolant shot up, spraying the stump of the dead man. The driver climbed out and ran to another tank.

The platoon had moved up, and Porter could hear Diemer and the tank commander talking above. "He what?" said the commander.

"He says link up. Link up. My Cherokee platoon's running out of ammo."

"Fucking Pie-in-the-Sky. Goddam, man, I can't move. They got mines, Mister! Nobody said they'd have mines. I got nine men dead and two tracks down. Link up? That sorry sack of shit."

Diemer dipped his forehead into a palm, pinched his temples with a thumb and forefinger. The muscles in his arms flexed. "They're gonna get chewed up," he said, accusingly. "They're gonna get chewed up."

"Can't move! Except back. Out of here."

Lieutenant Wolfe looked meaningfully at Porter, and Porter stepped back, understanding that all of this was not for his ears. But he heard Wolfe say, "I'll go in, sir. We'll get through."

He was volunteering!

Diemer shook his head, not in refusal, seemingly, but with an inability to consider. The battalion radio crackled with Jolly Green's voice and Diemer reached for the handset, like someone who's already on the phone.

Porter joined Preacher. "Turn around," he said; Preacher looked for Snowball, but Snowball stood at Wolfe's elbow, waiting respectfully. Signed on the dotted line, Porter thought. Didn't take much. Porter spun Preacher around and switched the radio to the battalion frequency. He held the handset so they both could hear.

". . . Gooks not move than one-zero-zero meters east your point vehicle. Plain as day up here. Running into your ambush element. But link up! Link up! I say again: you must link up. Cherokee has a body count of two-six, were you aware?"

". . . Negative," said Diemer.

"Roger. You're kicking ass, pardner! Now get your patrol out there; we got 'em nailed. We'll run some interference up here, so sit tight zero-four, then move when the shit lifts. How copy?"

"Solid copy."

"Jolly Green, out."

"What is it, Porter?" Preacher asked.

Porter switched back to the company frequency. "It's us, Preacher. It's us."

A Cobra gunship dove, firing rockets that trailed plumes of purple smoke. Two jets came screeching. Then it was almost quiet: the engines idling low, no small arms, rain soft as thought.

Snowball approached, looking guilty. He put something of their old intimacy into his voice, but Porter refused to respond. Snowball's eyes rose mournfully, and when they met Porter's, leaped with surprise. He stared between the columns of tanks. "You gots to point, Porter."

"Right," Porter said, and picked up his rifle.

Preacher stepped near. "I wish you were a Christian, Porter."

Porter looked at him, and opened his mouth to reply. But he couldn't.

*　　*　　*

It rained steadily. There was wind up high. The afternoon was nearly done: only a little firing came from Cherokee's direction now, none from behind him.

Once, when he dislodged its roost, a brightly-colored bird flew up at his face. He brushed the water from his eyes with a wet sleeve. He crouched, trying to see what lay ahead, fighting off something close to nausea. He hadn't realized how near to dark it was.

It might be that they were waiting until three or four had passed—they'd aim at Preacher because of his antenna, at Snowball because he was black. They hated black skin.

One thing: they would not have had the time to set booby traps.

Perhaps they were all gone, either dead or howling down a trail, cradling their wounds.

Porter moved forward another twenty meters. Further on he could see the barest indication of a path, a sort of tunnel through the foliage. In five more steps he discovered a sandal imprint, melting in the rain. Enough of guesswork: they were here still, one at least, hardly a minute ahead. With a flooded eye he traced a line forward, trying to establish that shadows weren't bodies. Perhaps the man was wounded, running from them like a gutshot deer . . . there was a burst of fire somewhere ahead, confirming the soldier's presence, possibly, or his death. Porter didn't want to go any further. He had spotted three small stumps, sawed off evenly.

He motioned and Okie slid noiselessly to his side. "Through there," Porter murmured, pointing toward the stumps. "That'll be the bunker complex. You see that footprint?"

"Yeah." Okie nodded. "Be an observation bunker maybe fifty, sixty feet. He might be in there." He pivoted on his toes and motioned to Snowball. He gestured left and right: a new man and

47

Billy Boy took positions looking out.

Snowball brought the machine gun down from his shoulder. "Know where they be?"

"Know where they *might* be," Okie whispered, motioning.

Porter could barely see. He was cold, slowly growing numb. He heard shouts a good distance behind, a deep groaning as the tanks turned around. There was no more firing, and the smoke had washed away. It was time to go: drink coffee, smoke cigarettes, read his mail.

"Bring in some artillery?" Snowball asked.

"Don't much want to," Porter said. "Can't see. We don't know for sure where Cherokee is: might hit 'em."

"No, no," said Preacher, pointing at his handset. "I talked to 'em: they got out the back way. Tanks went after 'em."

"Well," said Snowball. "Where Jolly Green?"

"He headed for Tay Ninh. Said he wasn't gonna fly around in the rain if we were done killing bad guys."

"Back at the messhall," Porter said. "Eating his curds and whey."

"Well, shit," said Okie. "Let's head on back. Get something to eat. Snow?"

"Good deal, Lucille," Porter said. "How about it, Preacher-Man?"

"Okay by me."

Snowball shook his head. "We can't, babes. Lieutenant Wolfe say we turn around, we turn around. You go on, Porter."

Porter couldn't believe it. "Go on, Porter?"

"You go on, now."

"Jesus H. Christ! I got sixty-three days. I don't have to listen to this shit. You goddam . . . *coon!*"

"Porter!" said Snowball. "You—"

"You blackassed motherfucking lifer. What the hell you—"

"Shut up, Porter," Okie said. "You cain't talk like that. Hush!"

"You lay off me, motherfucker!"

"Porter," said Preacher, tapping Porter's shoulder. "Porter. No. No."

Porter turned his face to the rain. He heard them rustling confusedly behind, and at length Okie squatted nearby, started to speak, didn't. Porter found a dry Pall Mall, but the rain hit it, and he threw it angrily away. Okie passed him a lit Winston; Porter cupped it carefully, took several long drags, passed it back. He glanced over his shoulder once, avoiding Snowball's eyes. Then Wolfe was bending at his shoulder. "What's the problem, Porter?"

"We're walking into bunkers."

"Cherokee killed a lot of gooks. What did you expect?"

"I saw a sandal imprint. It's got to be fresh, in all this rain. I'm not going anywhere."

"I been thinking, sir," Okie cut in. "Cherokee done got out, don't seem to be no reason to be on this patrol. Reckon we'll go on back?"

Wolfe bent his head, as though amused, and lit a cigarette beneath the bevel of his helmet. When he looked up it was through a wreath of smoke. "We have our orders. I'd like to go a little further."

"You could call up Captain Diemer, sir," Okie said. "I mean, here it is raining and going on dark. Anybody up there, Porter's right, they got us by the balls. We'll come back in the morning, sir. Be the whole company, daylight, tanks behind us."

Wolfe nodded as though to agree, but turned to Snowball. "How about it, Sergeant?"

The rain hung from Snowball's face, in drops that caught the waning light, and seemed silvery. He stared steadily at Porter. At last he said, "Maybe one or two gooks."

Wolfe smiled and grasped Porter's shoulder. He tilted his head to one side, like an understanding father. "What say, point man? Let's go a little further, what say?"

"It's suicide."

The Lieutenant shook his head, still seemingly amused; Porter could have struck him. "I don't think so, Porter. I think Cherokee drove them all off; we'll just run a little inventory while their shit is weak. Get any documents they left before they can come back tonight. All right?"

"Nosir. I'm not going any direction but backwards. I can't see. Maybe you'd like to point into those bunkers . . . sir."

Porter cocked his head; the Lieutenant lowered his, slowly released a breath. Cigarette smoke hung on his face, like a beard. His eyes were only dark places. "You know that's not my function, Porter."

"What is your function? To get me killed? I'm sick of this

teamwork crap, if I got to be the fucking football."

It was quiet. The insistent rain, the quickening darkness, merely shrouded them. Everyone stared at Porter; Preacher's face was incredulous, terrified.

The Lieutenant was rising. He cast his cigarette away. "All right, Porter. I'll point."

* * *

Surely no lieutenant in any army on earth was foolhardy enough to point. It was not what Porter had wanted. He had no interest in defiance. He had wanted someone to say, "You're right. Of course you're right." Now he felt robbed even of his minor status as a point man and would have shared in this lunacy. He fought an urge to run up from behind, take charge.

Wolfe was careful. He held his rifle as though it might shatter in his hands, and took steps only after he'd eyed every leaf. Several times, ignoring Porter, he motioned to Okie, for advice.

At last he reached the observation bunker. An arm lay atop it, at first seeming like a fallen branch. Wolfe kicked it away, dropped to the mud, and snaked over the bunker's roof—as he'd seen in the movies, perhaps, or learned in training. He held up a grenade and looked back at Porter, or so it seemed: faces no longer had expressions. Wolfe dropped the grenade through a firing portal, and somehow the muffled explosion took Porter far back, to that time he'd thrown a cherry bomb in the cistern. Even now he seemed eight years old, with his mother scolding him.

Wolfe stood and stared ahead, studying the dark buildings of the bunker complex. When he motioned, the men moved silently around him, fanning in a semi-circle. Porter could make out bags of rice beneath a shed, cutting tools, broken weapons, an open-air kitchen where the coals, still warm, spluttered in the rain. Snowball brushed past to set up the machine gun, and Porter moved near him, feeling lonely. He struggled, in the darkness, for a way to apologize.

"Spread out along the edge," whispered the Lieutenant roughly, the beginning of a cold bubbling in his throat. "Okie, Billy Boy, when they get in position, check for documents and weapons. Preacher, let me have that radio."

50

Porter remained behind it all, near Snowball. He began to speak, but couldn't. Billy Boy, unbelievably, paused to compliment Wolfe on his job of pointing; the Lieutenant waved him away. Holding Preacher's handset, with Preacher shivering at his side, Wolfe spoke to Porter across the dark space: "I'll bust you."

"I know it, sir."

Wolfe shook his head. "I don't understand. I thought you were born to point. No nerves. Loose. I thought you loved it."

Porter was sorry now. "Nosir, I—. How could anybody . . . like to—"

Wolfe cut him off with a wave of his hand. He brought the handset to his face, and his lips parted, probably to call Diemer. It seemed anticlimactic, a terrible cheat after all their caution. Three rounds popped out of the rain. Wolfe slumped and died.

Six more rounds: one of the new men fell, and Preacher died with a gurgle. Porter took a step forward. Had it happened?

"Down! Down! Down!" screamed Okie.

Snowball jumped behind the gun. Porter lay beside him, feeding ammo. Snowball fired fifty rounds, spraying wildly. What was the target? Bags of rice split open and peppered them. The belt grew short.

"Ammo! Ammo!" Porter yelled back, and two boxes came thudding at his feet. He reached around for them, and they were slick with mud, like flour paste, or grease, or blood. He turned to snap on a fresh belt, but Snowball lay still.

"Snow," Porter said. "Snow."

Porter rolled him over; he was bleeding at the neck. A hip was gone. Though his eyes were open, they were dark like the air, and Porter couldn't read them. "Snow?" Porter didn't know if Snowball saw him. "Snow?" Porter could have sworn that Snowball had grown pale now.

"The tree!" Okie was yelling, from ahead somewhere. "The fucking tree!"

Porter couldn't move. He knew which tree Okie meant; he realized that a man was firing at him. Of course the man *would* fire at the gun. It made sense, Porter thought, as Snowball bled on him.

Billy Boy leaped in beside him, clawing at bodies, pushing Snowball aside. He tilted the gun toward the tree. On and on now Billy Boy fired.

51

"Feed it!" Okie was screaming. "Porter, Porter, feed it!" So he did, clipping on another belt. Something fell.

"Hold it! Hold on," Okie said, standing.

Billy Boy kept firing.

"Stop it," Porter said. "Stop."

Billy Boy kept firing. Porter yanked at the belt, tore it apart. The gun jammed. "Billy Boy," Porter said.

Billy Boy was shaking all over.

*　　*　　*

Porter crawled into the personnel carrier as though into a cave. The gate whined up and then he couldn't see; his eyes didn't adjust. Tins of food rolled on the floor. Water sloshed against his boots and everything smelled like gasoline. Ahead somewhere the driver lit a cigarette, passed it to Okie. Porter was convinced they would explode.

They couldn't see, the blood made him slippery, and so it was impossible to hold him still. They hit a log, a clump of bamboo, something, and his head lurched into Porter's ribs. Porter changed hands, wiped them on his shirt, sought a dry grip. Once, he was certain, Snowball gasped. "That driver—"

"He cain't see," said Okie. "It ain't his fault, he cain't see."

"I wish we had him level. He's not level."

His body heaved—or it was the personnel carrier again, dropping into a hole, inching on.　"Going home, Snow," Porter said.

"Walking down the street," said Okie, "pretty girls everywhere you look . . ."

"Stay awake, Snow. Hear me? You just stay awake."

They had reached the field, although Porter didn't know this until the gate whined down and the night hit him with a burnt smell. They crawled out, and still Snowball kept slipping from them. Exhausted, they nearly dropped him on the wet grass. It was better then, with him on the ground and their hands free, no longer touching him.

It seemed like the end of someone else's battle; it seemed like the wrong place. Lights crisscrossed, blinding Porter. The rain crackled. Finally a man came toward them, jiggling a light. It played off the treetops, plunged deep into the jungle. Porter could see a great path diving jaggedly into darkness, but he did not believe that he had ever been there.

The medic trained his light down on Snowball, and bent to see. "I'm sorry," he said. "This fellow is dead."

*　　*　　*

All around the perimeter the armored and infantry had parted, as though there were shame in each other's company. The armored fired up their tapes of Hendrix and the Doors and disappeared inside the tanks. The infantry withdrew to the very center, and made a circle of its own.

A brand-new lieutenant, who'd flown out on the mail bird, came slogging through the mud to ask for the tank commander, but no one seemed to know where he was. The Lieutenant tried to talk to Captain Diemer, but Diemer wouldn't answer. Finally the Lieutenant withdrew. He hung at the fringes of various groups, then moved on again, unnoticed.

Captain Diemer was on the radio for a long time. His voice was shaky and self-conscious, as though he were auditioning for something. Occasionally he seemed angry.

His was the only voice that Porter heard, and it went on and on, like a recording. The Captain was trying to call in the names of the dead, but Battalion was too far away, the rain interfered, and he couldn't get through. "Say again," a voice at Battalion replied, clearly. "Read you weak and distorted." Diemer repeated the men's names. "Say again," said Battalion, more faintly, down a river of static. "Say again."

Joint after joint went around but it didn't make Porter sleepy, didn't make him float away. He walked around the perimeter, rubbing his neck. He ran into Okie. Okie handed him a perfumed letter, but they didn't speak. Porter tucked the letter away and forgot about it.

There was a surprise. The armored cook had made a great pot of bean soup, and put out a slab of Wisconsin cheese. Porter cut a piece of the cheese, grabbed some bread, and stuffed it all inside his shirt. He forgot about the cheese but continued walking the perimeter, sipping soup, smoking Pall Malls, staring into men's faces.

It was no use to think of Chris. He might as well have made her up, no more than he'd meant to her. He thought instead of Trudy, trying to put her into an agreeable fantasy, where when she opened her mouth it was only to say the precise and admiring thing he'd have her say. "Trudy, I'm home," he announced suddenly, as if to Rita Hayworth. It didn't help. He didn't know who Trudy was, what business she had in his mind. Trudy was dead. Everyone was dead.

"They run right at me," Billy Boy was saying. "Wouldn't stop. I said, I told Shari, I said I wasn't ever gonna shoot nobody, I said that." He began to giggle. Slowly everyone grew silent, watching him. Porter stopped, waited, stood just into the darkness beyond the circle of light thrown by a diesel candle. Billy Boy spun around, holding an imaginary machine gun: John Wayne. "Eh-eh-eh-eheheh!" he said. "Got 'em."

"Hush, now," said Okie.

"Eh-eh-eh-eheheh! This foot comes back at me?" Billy Boy kept giggling. Slowly Porter eased in from the dark, though he wanted to run away. "It was still in the boot, like. Laced up? Clean, how it come off. Isn't that weird? They just kept coming. Eh-eh-eh—"

Okie grabbed him. Billy Boy tried to fight, and swung his arms wildly. One of the new men, still a stranger to Porter, stepped in front of Billy Boy and slapped his face repeatedly, hard. Billy Boy slipped from Okie's arms down into the grass. "Mmmmmmmhmmmmmm," he said.

"Christ," Okie said, to the new man. "What you do that for? This ain't the fucking movies, troop."

Lightning quaked on the horizon. The rain had slowed to a drizzle, but the moon hadn't come out, and there would be no stars. Porter wrapped his poncho liner tightly around him, like a bandage. It had stayed dry. He lay down and pulled his poncho over his head. That was when he remembered his cheese and bread, and he munched on it deep down under, where no one could see him. When he opened his eyes the sun was shining, and the cheese lay by his hand.

Hot

Leon was in the air again. It was only in the air, when his head had cooled, that he could look around, breathe, and think of this life as a cycle. In the air he might remember how many days had passed, how many times the helicopters had come to carry him to an identical place, what else he'd done in his short life, who he was other than "Leon." The bird dropped suddenly, banking through haze. Nearly parallel to the ground, Leon imagined leaping away into flight. He'd glide down into one of those deep blue craters, fill his canteens, march away free ... the bird skimmed over a wide brown river now, nose down. "Where is it? Where we going?"

The doorgunner—with his helmet on, the radio in his ears—couldn't hear; unless he faced you, he couldn't read your lips. Now his problem anyhow. These men in the birds were aloof, a little mysterious with their sticks and gauges. It was as though they came not from some base but truly out of the heavens, moving round and round in the familiar air, like a freight train repeating its run. Leon would be standing there, ready to dissolve into vapors, when the machines pounced from the sky. Cold men in clean wool suits: moving parts. The gunner had turned, and Leon asked it again: "Where we going?" The man shrugged.

They dipped into a light rain, and the rotors pounded. They banked over a defoliated woods, with thick underbrush; a long field loomed. There was a radiance about the bird, a glow over all of them, and the rain had sun inside it, orange. This time, thought Leon suddenly. This is the one. So he screamed it: "Is it hot? Is it hot?" Meaning: will they shoot me today, will I lie by the crater full of drugs and dreams, will another bird take me away?

The gunner smiled. He sat erect on his perch, and tilted up

the machine gun. "Cold," he said at last, drawing out the word. "Cold."

*   *   *

As the company threaded into the darkening brush it was all Leon could do to keep Jackson, his squad leader, in sight. One boot chased the next. His head fell, and weariness bobbed along where sleep was supposed to be. Then the motion ceased, and he stood helplessly in the downpour as the others stretched the hooch, arranged guard, searched out dry matches for cigarettes. He flopped under the shelter, wrapped himself in his poncho liner. Everything was wet, but he fell asleep immediately, and was uplifted again, into fever and soft, radiant air.

In the bird around him were his mother and father, his older sister the lawyer, and Susan. The wind tore their words away. "What? What did you say?" he asked. But they all smiled and it seemed natural to be together, riding high, these people he loved and himself. The bird came out of mist, and the far-off horizon quaked with explosions. He was frightened. "Where we going?" he asked. "Please, where?" Susan pursed her lips in a "No," as though his question were in poor taste, as though he had violated her trust. Leon turned to his sister, who shook her head—knowing something, as she always had, that he didn't.

"Shhh." It was Jackson. "Hey, man. Your guard. Shhh."

The light went out. The rain thundered a few inches above; he crawled forward, trying to escape.

"What you doing. man?"

"I—"

"You sit right there. And stay awake."

". . . Anything?"

"That's a negative. You kidding, in this rain? I catch you sleeping again, Leon—"

"Not me." He was asleep instantly; from the bright air of his dream, emptied now of people, a place to cruise, he answered Jackson: "Yeah, yeah. I'm awake." He opened his eyes. It was like that experiment he'd read about, where they blindfolded you, put boxing gloves on you, and enclosed you in a padded chamber, to see what you'd do. You did nothing; you ceased to

56

exist. Better to dream, breathe in the wonderful light, fall away like a bomber into radiance.

*   *   *

In the dewy morning there was a boil under Leon's chin. It throbbed; already it was large as a golf ball and he felt it would keep growing, eat him up. Afterwards, the men would roll him down the trail.

"I had one of those on my ass," said the medic. "It'll bust."

"I can't go in?"

"The C. O. would never buy it, Leon. It'll bust. If it don't, come over again, two-three days, and I'll lance it."

Jackson looked at the boil and smiled. "You're losing it, Leon."

"The medic said it would bust."

"I tell you what I think: you better put in for R. & R. Go to Manila, forget the whores: just *sleep*. You're starting to be the jungle, man; it's taken root."

"I—"

"It's okay, Leon." Jackson sighed. "Want the bad news first?"

"Bad news?"

"You drew the point, and it's a long one. Can you do it?"

"What's the good news?"

"Hang in there, I'll pull your guard tonight."

"Oh."

"You fell asleep again, you know that?"

"I was awake. I—"

"I heard you snoring, man."

*   *   *

Leon backed into a tree, to take the pack's weight from his shoulders, and had a long drink. He massaged the boil, under his whiskers and hot skin: it would mash and move slightly, like clay, but then ooze back to its former shape. Cancer? So young, to die of cancer. He took the weight of the pack again, staggered briefly, plodded on.

Some part of him was still in tune with the temperature, the vagrant sounds, the treacherous path ahead. He detoured the open areas and nests of fire ants; he stayed on azimuth. There was a mood to the brush, a level of tolerable menace; if every piece of you were focused you could sense a change, something new, and you'd know to duck. But Leon was with Susan down by the lake. Her parents were at the door, and she hurried to gather her clothes, he his . . . he fingered the boil.

He stepped onto a broad trail the map hadn't shown. It was of hard-packed clay and there were fresh bicycle tracks. As it occurred to him he should consult Jackson an enemy soldier rounded a curve; instinctively, Leon raised his rifle. The safety was off and his finger on the trigger; he'd killed another man, months before, in precisely this situation. As the other man raised his rifle, briefly meeting Leon's eyes, in that instant when any prey freezes, Leon still didn't fire. It wasn't a choice, not mercy, not foolishness: he simply didn't fire. He was wondering where the enemy came from, it you could think there, eat a meal in peace, make love to a woman.

Jackson thrashed in the brush behind, and the enemy, sensing perhaps the entire company, turned and ran.

Jackson arrived. "You okay?"

"Yes." Leon searched Jackson's eyes. "Listen, I . . . I'm sorry."

"You're gonna get us killed." Jackson stared down the trail. "Just . . . go on. It's over; we're there."

"Where?"

"Here. The C. O. says spend the night."

*   *   *

Leon slept well enough, dry, dreamless. He awoke with first light, weak but calm, and sat squeezing the boil. "Coffee," he murmured.

"No time," said Jackson. "We gotta go."

"Where?"

"Meet some birds." He lit a cigarette. "I'm so goddam tired, Leon. How you doing?"

"I don't know."

"That thing's gonna bust."

58

Leon rose, and his weakness flooded him. The boil had swollen overnight, and his face felt bloated, his neck stiff. He made it to the field, his eyes on Jackson's boots. The birds were delayed and some of the men started coffee. Leon went away by himself, as though he would vomit; the others threw him sidelong glances. Jackson followed and stood at a polite distance. Leon knelt, pinched, and it rushed into his hands suddenly, a clot of yellowish goo and a little dribble of blood. Poison. Yet his chin had resumed its strange old shape. He felt intensely sleepy. He sat in the dirt, lit a cigarette for something to do, and then the cigarette was burning his fingers.

"You should go in," said Jackson, hovering like an angel. "Want me to talk to the Lieutenant?"

"What you say?"

"You're sick, Leon. You should go in."

"I don't—"

But here came the birds. They were so familiar that Leon was confused. They might go in reverse, and he'd develop the boil again, freeze at sight of the enemy.

Leon was in the air again! Air! In the cold air he expected to meet with his parents, with Susan, but there were only these strange men. "Short!" the doorgunner shouted. It was an announcement, as for weddings or babies. "Eight days!"

The gunner, Leon's acquaintance of dreams, was going home. He pulled iced Cokes from a cannister, passed out crackers and smoked oysters: a party at five thousand feet. Leon had liked oysters, but now, looking at them packed neatly in the tin, he might have retched. They were like what had come from his boil, his own rotten flesh. He closed his eyes, to contain his nausea, and in the cold air, with the bird rocking, he thought of his father, who used to swing him in the back yard, high enough to touch the summer moon. Leon opened his eyes and saw the bird's shadow, spinning on the clouds below, then plummeting to the ground. He knew they were coming down. "Where we going?"

The gunner shook his head. He adjusted his helmet and drew erect by the gun, took a swallow of Coke, spoke into the radio.

This time, thought Leon, this time. "Is it cold? Is it cold?"

The gunner lifted up the gun, cocked it. They were dropping fast. Jackson nudged Leon's shoulder, grasped his forearm. "It's hot, Leon."

"Hot?"

"Hot."

"Hot?"

Every man tensed, arranged his gear, pushed his feet out straight. The gunner began firing, aiming down at first, then locking his fire level into the woodline. The bird touched the grass, skimmed up a few inches, hovered.

"Out!" screamed Jackson. "Get the fuck out!"

"Oh God," said Leon. "Oh God oh God—"

"Leon, Leon—"

The machine gun rattled. The others were off, running low for cover, and now the pilot turned, jerked his thumb angrily. The machine gun stopped. Leon looked up. The gunner had slumped back, and bled below the chin.

"Leon, run!" Jackson screamed.

He did. Blat blat blat blat went the rotors, as the bird strained to rise, in the heavy air. Leon searched for Jackson, who could get him through.

"Leon, run!" But someone else had said it, because Jackson was dead. Leon rose, like a ghost out of his friend, and ran. He'd been here another time. He'd charged that same woods, done it all, done it again and again. Yet in the trees he saw what he hadn't before: one green shoulder behind the gun, like the corner of a dream or the hint of a new world. Another man fell. Leon stood erect—lightheaded, weary, sick—and raised his rifle.

The New Captain

By the time the old Captain was finished a third of us were dead or wounded, and the rest had been pushed so hard for so long that we were all nerves and suspicions, reduced to feeding our faces and hoping for one night's uninterrupted sleep. We went forty-three days without a hot meal or bath, until no one's skin was quite black or white or brown, but the green of mold and scum. Then, like a period of mourning, the old Captain was suddenly gone; we were standing in formation at Tay Ninh, saying goodbye. He saluted the Colonel and the new Captain, saluted us, and without a word stalked up the hill, toward a jeep piled with gear. He was a major now, en route to Germany.

The new Captain put us at parade rest and delivered his admonishments: there would be no drug use, he said, and no one would be allowed to get the clap. Captain John Sorley was not, however, a Billy Bad Ass. He respected us. Frankly, he was here because of his faith in America and in the American infantry, the finest group of men in the world. He'd volunteered for active duty and for combat because he was sick of what was going on back home; even his Guard unit had been full of malcontents. Standard stuff, though usually we heard more admonishments, less patriotism; patriots were rare as Christians. This one was plump and pushing forty: too old, you'd have thought, for war.

But then, at twenty-four, so was I.

I was an acting platoon sergeant—lieutenants kept getting killed right and left of me. Had it been a movie I would have been the quiet one, the veteran who seldom showed his emotions but was, under fire, cool and dependable. Not exactly, but none of the men I'd come in-country with were around to dispute my image. The truth was more nearly that my anger had so burned itself out that I hadn't anything left to say. What made me go was a desire to return home that ran so deep you might have called it delirium. Sorley would be my fourth captain; I could hardly respond when he came around, next day, to introduce himself. "Forty days to go, Jonesy?"

"Jones, sir, not Jonesy. Yes. Thirty-nine."

He stuck out a hand and then stood too near, so that I could smell his breath. It was sweet—and alcoholic. "Time to re-up!"

"I guess not, sir. I've made it this far—"

"You've done your duty. Where you from, son?"

"Arkansas."

He stepped back. In the scene he was playing, I should have been from Brooklyn or Texas, which would have bagged and tagged me: no need for further discussion. Apparently there was nothing to say about Arkansas. "Fine state," he mumbled, and moved on.

Late the following day two things happened: it began to rain, and my platoon received an order to fly out to an utterly forsaken rice paddy. We were to set up an ambush. This last was bad enough, but in the rain it would be miserable. It was an odd assignment, completely out of the blue, and I wondered if Sorley hadn't volunteered us.

Anyhow here he was, with two bandoliers and grenades strung from his ears, motioning impatiently toward the chopper pad down the hill a quarter mile. "C'mon, men," he shouted, waved a hand, and began to run. No birds were in sight, so I didn't run after him, and neither did the men. He turned, in anger and disappointment, and I guess it was the disappointment that made us pick up our feet. There was no need to hurt his feelings. We reached the pad, and at last the birds bore down over the hill.

Six inches of water covered the paddy. The pilots hovered two feet above it, while we slid down into the mud. Sorley led us to high ground, by a stand of denuded wild oranges. No one had been here since the French, I thought. It was nearly dark, and raining so hard you wondered there was space left to breathe.

We made a poor camp—simply snapping together our ponchos for hooches, and crawling under. It was too dark and wet to cook; I had a can of ham slices and some soda crackers. The ground was soaked. When at last a stream rolled into the hooch, we got up and dug a ditch. After that, things were tolerable; I rolled myself in my poncho liner like a cigar, and chain-smoked.

Toward midnight the rain stopped and the stars emerged, but

there was a cold wind. I'd sleep for awhile and then wake from some horrible dream: news my father was dead, or the discovery I had no legs. Sometime before the dawn there was a terrible crashing in the brush—I heard it in my sleep, grabbed my rifle, almost fired. It was Captain Sorley. He was excited, breathless. Could somebody be out there? I wondered. Here?

"Jonesy," he whispered.

". . . Yessir."

"We've got a man on the moon!"

"What?"

"It came over the radio. Right now! An American on the moon!"

"No shit, sir."

"Pass it on."

"Yessir."

I went back to sleep. In woods like these, I could have dreamed it all, awake or sleeping. Next morning, though, as we waited for the birds to return us for breakfast, I glanced at Sorley and thought: this one bears watching.

*　　*　　*

I had thirty-two days left when they dropped the company by a broad, nameless river, along which stretched forty miles and more of bamboo. No activity was reported, though six months before three battalions had chased an enemy regiment up and down the shore. Or the other way around, but in any case many had died.

It was beautiful country, to be so full of ghosts. The river ran quietly, a resolute traveling companion; the bamboo had not been bombed and was mammoth, virgin. Clumps of it had trunks eight and ten inches in diameter, a slick wet green that rose branchless for twenty feet and then sealed off the sky. The ground was even, with a deep layer of packed dry leaves; worms worked in rich dark soil. Sorley didn't move us far in a day, so that there was time to secure our hooches before the monsoon, to play casino or chess, write letters, dream. Suddenly I had twenty-eight days left, and my men regarded me with reverence almost, out of the certainty I was going to make it.

Sometimes we came upon evidence of the battle: a litter of C-ration cardboard, a circle of foxholes, or a bunker complex that must have served for a hospital. There were broken cots, mildewed bandages, decayed riggings for traction. The bamboo would be splintered and brown here, the sky would poke through; often deer browsed in the ruins. At each site Sorley fanned us in a circle and insisted on examining every shell casing and hooch pole. The time passed regardless. None of these ghosts could shoot.

He'd stride off inside the perimeter with Lieutenant Mason in tow, nodding, expostulating; he'd whirl suddenly and point; he'd kneel, trace the leaves with troop movements and strategy. Often we'd make camp early and send out patrols the remainder of the day, which—not at all in character for commanders— Sorley would lead himself, even taking the point sometimes, with his eyes narrowed and his jaw set. It was meaningless, of course, but that was no innovation.

Things were fine until the day my platoon had the point, and Screwy Louie found the snake. It was a python thick as a flagpole and twelve feet long, draped over the crotches of three clumps of bamboo. It was sluggish. Sorley came forward and stared for the longest time, but he hadn't a word. There was no point in bothering the thing, but abruptly—in his idea of impressing the new Captain or in veteran lunacy—Louie leaped forward with his machete and hacked behind the snake's head. It lashed about, busting up bamboo. Two others joined Louie with their own machetes, but the snake was tough, mostly bone, and moving besides, so that it took two or three minutes to sever its head. The thing came to ground somehow and went on thrashing. Sorley stumbled back, with a grin plastered over nausea. The company moved quickly, gratefully past.

And now the bamboo closed in. We had maps, every hour we calculated coordinates, but still we were lost. Your eyes couldn't penetrate the green for more than a hundred feet, and what you did see was clump after clump of bamboo, each clump identical. The branches arched above to form a tunnel that burrowed off in a dozen directions; I realized that I hadn't seen the sky for a week. Late in the day, the rain would fall on the mat above as on a roof, then drip through, down your back, into your eyes. The men trudged like the grey figures of a dream, seldom speaking and then only in whispers, their duties so deeply routine they went about them like zombies.

Night was worse. There might have been deer and monkeys, birds or buffalo, but you couldn't hear them: only the mumbling river, and the bamboo. No other sound like bamboo: creaking, chafing and moaning, shrieking with the rise of wind. Perhaps the moon shone oblong on the water or hung at an angle in the forlorn sky, and the bamboo would sound like men talking—zombies in the high branches, arguing in Vietnamese. I thought of my grandfather, lungs nearly finished with emphysema, out on his front porch rocking on the pine floor, creaking . . . then, with an effort, I could shut it out, sleep. No one was there. Yet I'd wake and the wind would have ceased and the leaves would throb with moonlight and above the river's sound there would be silence, and I'd wait, and the bamboo would creak again, once. Oh, it could not matter, I'd tell myself, yet I'd sit awake until the dawn, cupping my cigarette, shivering.

It was on such a night, fifteen days down the river, when Sorley's nightmares began. My mind that morning had merged with the river, in that drugged state between wakefulness and sleep, and I had no thoughts, only the river within me, stifled feelings receptive to terror: "Oh . . . " moaned the Captain. Then he shouted it: "Granville! Is that you?" I rose, and with Lieutenant Mason stumbled toward his position. "Sir. Sir," the Lieutenant hissed. "Please, please. No."

"I'm sorry," the Captain said.

It went on for the next several nights, in the silences before dawn; I'd slip over with Mason and the medic, and hold Sorley by his shoulders. "Don't tell anybody about this, Jonesy," he'd say. Sometimes he screamed like a wounded man, and you wanted to shoot him full of morphine. "Shhh. Hush, sir. Not here," the Lieutenant told him, in a hoarse whisper.

"Did I do it again?"

"We *have* to be quiet, sir."

"A dream. I'm all right now. My uncle, his name was Granville—"

"Granville, sir," I said. "Hush."

"He only had one arm. He used to try to hug me, and it scared me, when I was a kid . . ."

"In the morning sir," said Mason.

What the medic gave him helped, but still in the daytime Sorley's face was swollen as from a sting, and his eyes, which seemed tiny and deep, were bloodshot. You could see him laboring to hide a kind of guilt, reaching out to any man who'd look at him in an appeal for understanding—patience, forgiveness. But the men had ceased to believe in him, if they ever had; they avoided his eyes.

There was nothing in these woods, we told him. Bamboo was just like that: full of spooks. He said he knew it, that he'd lost his confidence briefly, simply lost his bearings. He called me Jonesy but seemed, as the sedative overtook him, to confuse me with his son. His son was in college, and a draft resister. How was it, Sorley lamented, that a man who had belonged to the union, who had served in the Guard for seventeen years, could raise a son who was a draft resister?

One night I pulled the last guard, the one ordinarily hardest to stay awake through. I remember propping myself up, getting a light from the medic and then cupping my cigarette, settling into a state just above dreams, and thoughts perhaps of an old girl friend; there was no sound but the isolated snap and slow fizz as someone opened a beer. Then there was a loud crack as of a limb breaking, and a splash.

Sorley had risen and walked noiselessly to the shore. It was a miracle he hadn't drawn fire, but no one had even seen him. He was shouting now. "Lights! Lights!"

The medic and I hurried to find him, across the glimmering leaves. Mason was already there, in the water beside him; they glowed in the moonlight. I helped them to shore. "Shut up!" Mason said, when the Captain began to protest.

"Lights," Sorley explained. "Don't you see the lights, Jonesy? Over there, across the river, in the bamboo there. That's where they are—all this time."

"It's the moon, sir," I told him.

"We've got to report this. Call in artillery. Lieutenant—"

"It's just the moon, the moonlight," I said. "You see things that aren't there. They wouldn't give themselves away like that—they wouldn't use lights. You never see them, sir. Calm down, now. Please."

"Don't they . . . go in boats?"

"Nosir."

"Oh." He let himself be guided back to his position, where we laid him down, covered him. Sleepwalking, I thought, but then it hit me that it wasn't merely that. It wasn't simply nightmares; it wasn't madness. It was just fear, all mixed up with his uncle and the son who'd taken a forked path, perhaps too his desire to count for something, to go home a hero.

That was the end. Lieutenant Mason was whispering violently on the radio. He woke up the Colonel.

*   *   *

I remember rolling from side to side, maybe even crying out, as though someone were beating me. When I woke, I didn't know where I was. A good old boy and a soul brother were arguing over possession of the pool table. No harm could come: this was the Red Cross Club. A Doughnut Dolly looked at me in a sort of apology, and I smiled. She spoke to the soldiers in a tone meant to inspire guilt over abuse of a privilege. "Fuck her," one said. "You gots to be an officer," said the other.

I went into the sun. It was late afternoon; a gritty wind had risen, shriveling every live thing. The air conditioning, the dream, only made me more tired. It was a mile to the mess hall, down a baked red road: I wiped my face with a towel and forced myself into a faster pace. Only four more days, I thought.

I hadn't walked far when a lieutenant with the markings of finance gave me a ride. He nodded, but said nothing. He was neat and clean in a way I'd forgotten how to be; even those dull, Korean-made boots were shining. I watched those boots trying to speed-shift the jeep: this had been the war for him. Mortar rounds to either side, and, like Rock Hudson, he had to get us through.

He stopped on the hillside above my company area. How could he know where I lived? "Good luck to you, Jonesy," he said.

"Thanks, I will," I said. I will what? The mystery of how he could know me without my knowing him put me at distance from myself. I stood, disoriented, as he drove away.

There was a formation below. In the heat everything swirled, but gradually I saw that it was supposed to be my company. They had gone to the field two days before, so that this group was nothing but cooks, clerks, medics, and of course the shammers—those with minor wounds or the clap, those who got high and stared all day at the ceiling. Bodies, to stand more or less erect, and make a ceremony. What ceremony? There had been no announcement in the morning. I crouched on the hillside, my back to the glare and the desiccating wind, a spy. There was a pale quarter moon low on the horizon, strafed with grit.

Here were the Colonel, Captain Sorley, and a new captain I didn't recognize—a soul brother in starched fatigues, dazzling boots. The Colonel began to speak but then six birds churned low overhead, bound for the jungle. Their noses dipped in formation, with the moon between them and the sun glinting off their rotor blades: lovely.

I understood. The Colonel finished his speech and saluted the black captain, who saluted Sorley and then began spitting out admonishments to his stoned troops.

Walking stiffly, but with his trousers too high and his back slung forward, Sorley accompanied the Colonel up the hill, toward a jeep piled high with gear. He saw me, and I stood, wondering if I should salute. "Sir," I said, and stepped back, thinking: he's drunk. Was he drunk? Did he need to be? He stared at me for a moment, as though I were from another world. Then, without a word, he jerked up his head and moved on.

Gomez

Long after his hitch as a warrant officer, after time served as a parts clerk, an orderly, a cashier, Danny Gomez found himself out of work. With nowhere to go, nothing to buy, he explored the city.

There were farmers selling peaches from trucks, and flea markets, and massage parlors. There were old men with a mean look, cruising in big cars with rolled-up, tinted windows. There were fat women at motel swimming pools. Mostly there was traffic, nervous, stifling, endless: his generation, passing him by.

He walked into the country, down the all but forgotten railroads. It amazed Gomez how, in no more than thirty years of neglect, nature could reassert itself. At night, not a train would pass as he slept in the scrub oak. Owls flew; deer slipped down below the bridges to drink the dirty water.

Gomez was happy then; he remembered his father. The old man would have liked it by the tracks. These hills were nothing like the bleak Sonora desert where Gomez was born, nor the manicured desert, Riverside, where he had grown up. The hills were green, full of water and wildlife—or, if he left the tracks, modular homes, hobby farms, gift shops with ceramic frogs on the grass.

One day an ad appeared in the paper, describing, surely, no one but Gomez: "City man desires groundskeeper and house manager for country retreat. Applicant must be in good health and a qualified helicopter pilot. Quarters, good salary."

The city man was an old lawyer named Harris. He was a local fellow who had worked his way through school, returned to the city, and eventually, as an outgrowth of his practice, been elected to the state senate. He had more money than he knew what to do with, which he'd made, Gomez learned, not with law but real estate. "Drink?" Harris asked.

"No, thank you."

69

Harris nodded slowly, studying Gomez. "Wait 'till I'm gone, huh?"

"I don't drink." It never occurred to Gomez to be insulted; he stood quietly, in his tie, brown shirt, and no coat, hands folded in front of him.

Harris coughed, and his tone went higher. "This is where I spend my money," he said, motioning through a sliding glass door toward the wooded hills. There were more than seven hundred acres. "Some friends of mine like to come out here and let down their hair. I had the park service introduce some Rio Grande turkeys, so the hunting's good. Got lineside bass stocked in that lake you passed, coming in. It's springfed."

Harris stared at Gomez out of eyes that bulged slightly. Gomez cleared his throat. "Good water—that's always important."

The lawyer frowned and rose to mix another drink. He turned quickly. "Some very important people come here. We drink. We play some cards. Right here is where, you want my personal opinion, the parks bill was passed."

Gomez glanced through the glass door. "Oh, yes. The parks bill."

Harris laughed. "Never heard of it, have you? That's the way it is. Man works his balls off on a major piece of legislation, and they never heard of it. What your father do, Mr. Gomez?"

"He was a gardener. That's how I learned—"

"Was he a poor man?"

Gomez stiffened. "Yes."

"I used to be a poor man. Well, Mr. Gomez, you'd have it to yourself here. Keep the grass mowed, spray the roses and the pear tree, vacuum in here, make the beds, rustle up breakfast, mornings where there's people. Ah, sometimes there's ladies, you know; wanta be careful, you don't talk around. Keep things stocked up: food and spirits. Mostly breakfast, like I said. We'll run into town for supper. You handle all that, Gomez?"

"Yes."

"You got a gal friend?"

"No, sir."

"Gonna say, you got a gal friend, bring her out during the week. No problem."

"Thank you."

70

"You don't—well. We'll get acquainted. First off, now, you fly me into town. Bought a little Bell Model E, not twenty hours on the overhaul. Runs nice. I used to fly, got too old, bad heart." Harris stared again. "I think this job oughtta go to a quiet fella."

Gomez was alarmed. "I'm very sorry. I don't see many people; I'm not . . . in practice."

They walked to the pad. A silence built as Gomez fumbled with the controls, remembering them. The last time he'd flown one of these, he was carrying three dead ARVN's to their families in Bien Hoa. It was early morning, after a rain. Around the compound, the barbed wire glistened.

"You talk about the parks bill. Yes, I do have my doubts, but land use, my God, that's the whole show now. Got to be too damn many people. You want privacy, well, you gotta buy in. I tell you, Gomez, damn thing wouldn't have passed on our side if it wasn't gonna screw up the Federal funding. Fucking Federal government. Some very important people have been out here, Gomez."

"Yes, sir," said Gomez, loudly, easing the chopper up off a bubble of air. "I imagine that's so."

*   *   *

How many years passed? The hills didn't change; if anything the streams ran purer, the bass leaped higher. Gomez worked weekends; he worked Mondays cleaning up and replenishing. The rest of the week was his, to walk or fish or read.

The little he did was more than enough for Harris: Gomez was a passable cook, a good bartender, and, down the trails he'd cut through the woods, the most attentive of guides for the florid, middle-aged men and the stunning young women.

Sometimes one of these important men would grow very drunk, vomit it all up, and fall asleep. More than once, when Gomez had tucked him in bed, the sick man's woman would make a pass. It put Gomez in a bad place. Why, if such a woman sought power or luxury, would she turn to him? He was a small man, athletic but not "handsome." Strange as it seemed, Gomez decided that such women liked the color of his skin, brown but not black and therefore not quite so recklessly exotic. The

71

women did not seem quite real to Gomez. Yet he couldn't anger them: they could whisper in an important man's ear; the important man could have his job. If things grew too close, too desperate (the sick man snoring in the same room), Gomez made his English bad and said, "I am sorry. I have a sickness." Then the woman would hurry downstairs, controlling a blush.

He bought a compound bow and shot it into a target each morning. His arms grew strong. He shot turkeys and baked them on Saturday nights, when there were enough people. The turkeys were stupid. Still, in flocks, they had cunning, and he delighted in waiting for them, with his thoughts, his memories, at a standstill. Hidden away, a perfect citizen of the woods, he felt complete.

Perhaps he was two men. One—the waiter, the pilot, the gardener—sought only to serve. Friendly, accommodating, he could provide intelligent conversation if it were required; he could give assurance that the world was coming around to one's own way of thinking.

"Why'd we lose that war, Gomez?"

"Because we didn't believe we were right."

Or: "Ask me, we should have bombed Hanoi in '64."

"It would have been the merciful thing to do."

The other Gomez understood the war no more in reflection than when he'd fought in it. Important people brought it up, in a way, to be polite; really it meant nothing, it was a dead issue.

More than anything else, that other Gomez wanted to be left alone. He wanted noise only if it were a tom gobbling, tree frogs chanting. *How are you how are you how?* they sang. *I'm fine fine I'm fine fine* came a reply. Tuesday through Friday, Gomez sat on the bluff above the lake, staring through the blue haze above the hills, toward the city.

*   *   *

In a year, ten years, the important people no longer came, and the chopper set idle. Harris was no longer important; he was merely old. For months he did not come at all, and then, suddenly, he was there to stay. He lay dying. Attesting to how important he must have been, a doctor came to examine him twice a week, and whispered instructions to Gomez.

Gomez fed Harris, gave him his medicine—and mixed the strictly forbidden drinks. He tuned in the television. Propped up, Harris drank until he reached his plateau, and then his eyes held to the screen until he had fallen asleep again.

Gomez had more time alone than ever, yet something was wrong. He didn't miss the parties, the conferences, nor did he care very much about Harris. But a new feeling, a sort of bewilderment, tugged at him.

The small town where twice a month he had gone for groceries and bait had suddenly closed down. The houses were boarded up, the school's windows broken out, and weeds grew high. Over there the cattle ran, there the spindly corn grew (Gomez had always wondered why they farmed the land at all)—but there also was an abandoned farm, and two unoccupied ranchstyles, with "No Trespassing" posted.

Was there such a surplus in the big farm states to the north that marginal operations like these had at last been forced out? Was a dam going in that would flood the town? He searched the papers, watched the news on television. No, nothing was wrong. Children were going to school; taxes were going up. A councilman was being recalled. He drove to another town for supplies, on the edge of the city, and all was fine. He stopped at McDonald's—and yes, there were still Big Mac's.

One night a month later he was awakened by a shotgun blast. A group of men stood in the yard, a large flatbed truck behind them. They seemed old. The shotgun burst again and knocked the glass from the sliding door. Gomez leaped to the den for Harris's .30 .30; lying on the carpet, rifle pointed toward the broken door, he dialed the police.

"Harris, you pig-eyed bastard!" one man screamed.

Gomez fired two rounds over their heads, and they stumbled back against the truck. One man was drunkenly laughing and crying at the same time; another tried to console him.

Upstairs, the television was playing.

Another scream: "Harris!"

Gomez, staying out of the light, yelled: "Go away. He's dying. He can't even get out of bed."

The men milled silently.

"I've called the police."

They left then, cursing, throwing a sack of cans on the porch. Gomez walked outside and sat on the steps, shaking. When the police arrived, and he couldn't describe any of the men, they were furious. "What you do here, pal?"

"I'm the caretaker."

"My opinion, you got no business out here at all. Kinda people out in the night, these days? They'd as soon shoot as look at you."

"We've never had any trouble."

The troopers roared off down the lane. On the farm-to-market road, their red light and siren came on; perhaps they had spotted the truck.

Gomez hurried upstairs. He shut off the television, controlling his anger. He said to Harris, "Had you harmed these men?"

"Never saw 'em before." Harris moved his head with great effort. "Turn on the tv."

"But—man—people don't act that way."

Harris sighed. "Oh. Maybe somebody has a farm, ain't worth nothing, only he thinks it is. Take a farm like you got in Io-way, that black soil goes down, hell, ten foot, and good farmers, they got the machinery, banks behind 'em now, they gonna farm, that's right. Oh but well, you got a Federal grant. You see? Gomez, in this country, we have the separation of powers. We have the church and we have the state. So you make it a park. Might as well, or you gonna farm, well, by God let's farm. Don't pussyfoot around, Gomez. I'm thirsty. Well now Lord, there is the right of eminent domain. Always been legal, always will. Say you some doctor, businessman, St. Louis, wanta get out. Understannable. Want some pissant farmer hogging the woods? Worse thing still, all these double-wides, junk cars, and the septic tanks leaking in the springs? Fucking up the streams, Gomez? Ah, thank you, Gomez."

He let the old man drink the water, then gave him a pill. "They take a man's land?"

"Raise the taxes, buy him out. Wouldn't you, in this country?"

"Push a man into the city."

Harris was trying to sleep. He would have his dreams again, Gomez saw; he'd be up half the night with him. "I don't believe it," Gomez said.

74

Harris had gone white. "Compensation. A man will be staked in the city; he will find a job." Harris was helf-asleep, yet excited, as though beginning to dream, now, of his youth. "There's always compensation, Gomez—"

"Of course," said Gomez, tucking the blankets around the old lawyer's very white, caved-in chest.

*   *   *

Harris died two weeks later, only hours after his visit from the doctor. Gomez walked in the woods, thinking, I'm forty-one, no, forty-two. It was mid-morning. Below the small dam, beaver had returned; a few days before, Gomez had surprised a bobcat. He hated Harris. Gomez's own father had never owned land.

He loaded the body onto the chopper and flew to the city. After he'd tied the machine down, a policeman greeted him. "See your blue card?"

"This is old Senator Harris. He died this morning. I'm supposed to contact a Judge Monroe."

The policeman nodded. "Well, yeah. He was quite the old fella, wasn't he? Look—ah, don't you have the blue card?"

"What? I don't understand."

"I'm sorry. I'm sposed to ask. You can get one there in the terminal, no big deal."

"What is it?"

"I don't know, exactly—I'm just sposed to ask. They just started doing it. See, you can go out, if you're having a picnic or something, once you got the blue card. I don't hardly see how they could hold you, anyways. Take too many men, don't you think? Hell—" He pointed to the woodline at the end of the runway. "—see there? Kids playing outside the wire, there. They didn't even put it up good."

"That's . . . wire?"

"Well, sure."

"That's concertina wire!"

"You figure out City Hall, Mister, you're smarter than me. I—"

Gomez nodded. The policeman walked back inside for a cup of coffee, embarrassed. Gomez made his call, and then stood by the chopper. The wire stretched around the airport, down the horizon into the woods—only one coil. Anyone could get through, he thought. Why put it up?

In an hour an ambulance arrived, carrying the judge. "You're this Gomez?"

"Yes."

"Did he suffer?"

"No. I don't think he suffered."

"Go out in his sleep?"

"He was watching tv. It was very quiet."

"Well, I'll take care of things here. You'll have to go out again and shut down the house—no livestock, was there?"

"Just a cat."

"Good. You'll want to move into the city—couple weeks, come on around. I'll find you a job."

"I thought—well. Thank you. Sir."

The judge smiled and stepped back into the ambulance; Gomez turned away. The judge rolled down a window. "Gomez, you have the blue card? I know you've been isolated."

"I—"

"Better get a temporary, at least."

*   *   *

Two weeks passed, and a third. The telephone went out, the electricity went off, the gas company came for its tank. Gomez drained the pipes, boarded the windows, locked the doors. He stayed in the toolshed, heating spaghetti and meatballs on a wood stove. Once he started the chopper, but shut it off again. He went to the woods, shot a turkey with his bow, wished he hadn't.

In the fourth week a woman from the park service drove up in a Toyota. "Why did you board the windows?"

"I thought—"

"It's all right. This will be a sort of clubhouse here, that's why I asked. Fishing, hunting. Sir, who are you?"

"My name is Danny Gomez. I worked here."

"I'm Shirley. I'm really sorry, Mr. Gomez, but the property belongs to the state now, and I have to ask you to leave. You'll be going in to Springfield—or St. Louis or Kansas City, if you'd prefer that."

"Of course. Just—some details, took longer than I thought they would. I'll be leaving in the morning."

"I'm sure you'd be able to use the club yourself, if you wished, after you worked here and all."

Gomez nodded slowly as she drove away. But in the morning he didn't leave: it was a beautiful day, and he sat by the lake, watching the fish take the insects on the water's surface. Night fell; another day passed, and then, not long before dawn of the next day, a state police car slid up the lane, carrying two troopers. Lights out, they drove slowly around the house; Gomez woke to the sound of the engine. He dressed quickly. The men came toward the shed, calling his name. The harsh voices, as though from a dream, panicked him; he grabbed the bow and quiver and slipped toward the woods.

"Gomez!"

"Yes," the good servant in him answered, "I'm here."

The troopers' light cut toward his voice, caught him standing. "All right, Mr. Gomez. You were asked to leave, and you've refused to go. If you'll come with us, please?"

He could not have explained it, yet something made him leap away from the light and into the woodline. Caught by a blackberry briar, he thrashed clumsily, cut himself.

"You—" The troopers' light plunged wildly around Gomez. "Come out or I'll have to shoot. Listen. You think you can do anything with that bow and arrow, fella—"

Gomez tore free of the briars and crunched further back. He was making too much noise. "Stupid bastard," said one of the troopers, and fired his revolver into the air. Gomez broke into a sweat. He raised the bow. Knowing the trooper had not tried to shoot him, but no longer reasoning—terrified, yet physically calm, he let fly an arrow at the jiggling light. The trooper fell.

"Good Christ!" said his partner, and fired without aiming, hitting to Gomez's right. Gomez shot toward the sparks from the revolver.

And that man was dead, too.

*   *   *

77

He took the time to drain the gasoline from their car; there was not much left in the chopper. He packed tins of food in a gunnysack and rigged a pack. He broke into the house for the rifle and single box of ammunition. The arrows in the men sickened him; he left the bow.

The chopper ran poorly. Flying low, he passed over Lake Taneycomo, and turned west, over the hills, away from towns. In Arkansas or eastern Oklahoma the chopper began losing power on the low-octane fuel, and he set it down on a deserted gravel road. He had quickly memorized the terrain from the air, and now struck south, through a dry woods, until he reached a railroad. Weeds grew in the tracks; here and there a tree was starting.

He built a fire and slept until it had gone to coals. He heated some beans and drank water. He tied the gunnysack to his pack, shouldered the pack, and carried the rifle in his hand.

He walked the rails, or alongside them in the weeds. There was no aircraft overhead, and at the crossings there were no cars. After a time the inside of him began to settle down. The tracks, he thought, were pointing toward Mexico.

Lisa

Roy was walking across the commons when he saw her. She wore old clothes and sandals, as she always had, and her hair still reached to her waist. She was across the street, by the Engineering building; miraculously, her eyes caught his across the bobbing heads of the crowd, but then she turned away. She walked faster, downhill, away from him. "Lisa!" he shouted.

He began running, but it drew attention to himself. With his short hair, he might as well have been naked. He leaped up, waved, shouted, but she didn't turn, and now a soldier was eying him. There had been riots for several nights and soldiers were on the roofs, at every entrance, on corners; violence seemed to hang above the crowd, gathering slowly, shaping itself for the dark. They might think he was a killer. The boys and girls might knot up suddenly, hunch him against a building, beat him to death. It was his hair: he could have been on the roof. Otherwise, otherwise . . .

He had reached the street. Lisa was halfway down the hill now, and he hurried on the opposite sidewalk, dodging bodies, ignoring the curious, uplifted eyes . . . no friends here. Insane to think so, and a mistake to come, three days removed from war: no old girl friends in the phone book now, and his roommates were in grad school, teachers, dentists. Just one moment, and Lisa would know him, throw her arms around him . . . he called out. Cars rushed by, but he knew she'd heard him. There was a hint of hypocrisy about her back, and a guilty arc in the air between them. "Lisa!"

Roy's weariness washed over him. He should have gone home, gone to his father; he was asking for trouble here. How could Lisa be so cruel, to ignore him, pretend he didn't exist? All because he'd been a soldier . . . he began running again. Those coming up the hill parted hastily, and stared in alarm. Perhaps too the soldiers, watching from the roofs for the unusual, trained

79

eyes and rifles down on him now; at any moment a machine gun would strafe across his legs. "Lisa!"

He ran onto the street; a car braked sharply and the driver scowled. Everyone, everyone but Lisa spun about and stared. "Hey!" he shouted, behind her now. Down in front of the library two soldiers stood together, talking, smoking. They stared at him too, this odd figure, broken-field running among the boys and girls. He'd passed her. He wheeled, walked backwards. "Lisa? Lisa, what's the idea? It's me, Roy!"

"Hi, Roy," she said mockingly.

"Don't you know me?"

"Know you? Am I supposed to? No!"

"Lisa. Please, please, Lisa. We were . . . friends. I wrote you . . . letters. Don't you, please, don't you remember?"

She was serious now. "No. I'm not Lisa, I'm Sondra. I don't know you, whoever you are. I don't know you!"

"No! You're Lisa! I know you, you—"

A little crowd milled on the sidewalk—bemused, pitying. Roy stood at the curb, speechless. The woman was very much like Lisa, freakishly like her, same hair, same eyeshadow. But the nose, perhaps, was longer, and the skin fairer. Not her. "I guess . . . I'm sorry. I don't know you." Someone in the crowd laughed.

"It can happen," the woman said. "Mistakes." There was a tone in her voice, worried, gentle, healing, that seemed familiar. "Are you okay?" she asked. "Will you be all right?"

"Sure." He rubbed a hand across his short hair. "What?"

She turned down the hill. Not Lisa, though she was the same height, had the same hair, walked the same. Not Lisa, but he recognized her shirt. She turned once more, with a stare, a forbidding smile. Behind, the two soldiers broke apart to either side of her. And Roy looked through a little crevice in her eye, as though he were sunshine, breaking into a dark room. Deep in there was a wildness he knew, the key to everything. Wasn't it Lisa? Could you forget the eyes of a woman you'd made love to? "Oh," he murmured, as she fled from him. "Oh, I don't know you, I don't know you, I don't, I don't. Lisa!"

Other Books From BkMk Press

Artificial Horizon, by Laurence Gonzales. Short stories. $8.95.

Missouri Short Fiction, edited by Conger Beasley, Jr. 23 stories by Missouri writers. $7.95.

In the Middle, edited by Sylvia Griffith Wheeler. Poems and essays by ten Midwestern women poets. $8.95.

Modern Interiors: lithographs & confessions, by Stephen Gosnell. $12.95

Writing in Winter, poetry by Constance Scheerer. $5.25.

Selected Poems of John Knoepfle. $6.50.

The Selected Poems of Mbembe Milton Smith. $8.95.

Dark Fire, By Bruce Cutler. A book length narrative poem. $6.25.

From BkMk's Translation Series

Wild Bouquet, by Harry Martinson (Swedish Nobel Laureate). Poetry and original drawings by the poet. Introduction by William Jay Smith. Translated by William Jay Smith and Leif Sjoberg. $10.95

A Charles Guenther Sampler, poems translated from Eskimo, Greek, Hungarian, Italian, French and Spanish.

Hi-Fi and False Bottom, by Goran Stefanovski. Two plays by a well-known Yugoslavian playwright, translated from the original Macedonian, with an introduction by James McKinley. $8.50